ECONOMICS FOR MANAGER

Dr. Himanshu Raninga

ECONOMICS FOR MANAGER

PREFACE

THE NEED

Economics is required for effective resource management was put in place due to the following developments in the global business environment:
 (a) Growing complexity of business decision-making processes.
 (b) Increasing need for the use of economic logic, concept, theories, and tools of economic analysis in the process of decision-making.
 (c) Rapid increases in the demand for professionally trained managerial manpower.

These developments have made it necessary that every manager aspiring for good leadership and achievement of organizational objectives be equipped with relevant economic principles and applications. Unfortunately, a gap has been observed in this respect among today's managers. It is therefore the aim of this course to bridge such gap.

This book is aimed to :

On reading of this book students and managers alike will be expected to:
1. Understand the relative importance of Economics;
2. Know how the application of the principles of managerial economics can aid in the achievement of business objectives;
3. Understand the modern managerial decision rules and optimization techniques;
4. Be equipped with tools necessary in the analysis of consumer behaviours, as well as in forecasting product demand;
5. Be equipped with the tools for analyzing production and costs;
6. Understand and be able to apply latest pricing strategies;

ECONOMICS FOR MANAGER

UNIT 1: DEFINITION AND IMPORTANCE OF ECONOMICS

Content
1.0 Introduction
2.0 Objectives
3.0 Definition and Importance of Managerial Economics
3.1 Definition of Managerial Economics
3.2 Importance of Managerial Economics
3.3 Scope of Managerial Economics
3.4 Managerial Economics and Gap between Theory and Practice
3.5 Self-Assessment Exercise
4.0 Conclusion
5.0 Summary
6.0 Tutor-Marked Assignment
7.0 References

1.0 Introduction
The discovery of managerial economics as a separate course in management studies has been attributed to three major factors:

3. The growing complexity of business decision-making processes, because of changing market conditions and the globalization of business transactions.
4. The increasing use of economic logic, concepts, theories, and tools of economic analysis in business decision-making processes.
5. Rapid increase in demand for professionally trained managerial manpower.

It should be noted that the recent complexities associated with business decisions has increased the need for application of economic concepts, theories and tools of economic analysis in business decisions. The reason has been that making appropriate business decision requires clear understanding of existing market conditions market fundamentals and the business environment in general. Business decision-making processes therefore, requires intensive and extensive analysis of the market conditions in the product, input and financial markets. Economic theories, logic and tools of analysis have been developed for the analysis and prediction of market behaviours. The application of economic concepts, theories, logic, and analytical tools in the assessment and prediction of market conditions and business environment has proved to be a significant help to business decision makers all over the globe.

2.0 Objectives
At the end of this unit, you will be expected to:
1. Have an understanding of the meaning and importance of managerial economics
2. Understand the relevant phases in business decision making processes

3. Be familiar with the scope of Managerial Economics
4. Be able to discuss freely how managerial economics can fill the gap between theory and practice

3.0 Definition and Importance of Managerial Economics

3.1 Definition of Managerial Economics

Managerial economics has been generally defined as the study of economic theories, logic and tools of economic analysis, used in the process of business decision making. It involves the understanding and use of economic theories and techniques of economic analysis in analyzing and solving business problems.

Economic principles contribute significantly towards the performance of managerial duties as well as responsibilities. Managers with some working knowledge of economics can perform their functions more effectively and efficiently than those without such knowledge.

Taking appropriate business decisions requires a good understanding of the technical and environmental conditions under which business decisions are taken. Application of economic theories and logic to explain and analyse these technical conditions and business environment can contribute significantly to the rational decision-making process.

3.2 Importance of Managerial Economics

In a nutshell, three major contributions of economic theory to business economics have been enumerated:

1. *Building of analytical models* that help to recognize the structure of managerial problems, eliminate the minor details that can obstruct decision making, and help to concentrate on the main problem area.
2. *Making available a set of analytical methods* for business analyses thereby, enhancing the analytical capabilities of the business analyst.
3. *Clarification of the various concepts used in business analysis*, enabling the managers avoid conceptual pitfalls.

3.2.1 Economic Analysis and Business Decisions

Business decision-making basically involves the selection of best out of alternative opportunities open to the business organization. Decision making processes involve four main phases, including:

Phase One: Determining and defining the objective to be achieved.

Phase Two: Collection and analysis of information on economic, social, political, and technological environment.

Phase Three: Inventing, developing and analyzing possible course of action

Phase Four: Selecting a particular course of action from available alternatives.

Note that phases two and three are the most crucial in business decision-making. They put the manager's analytical ability to test and help in determining the appropriateness and validity of decisions in the modern business environment. Personal intelligence, experience, intuition and business acumen of the manager need to be supplemented with quantitative analysis of business data on market conditions and business environment. It is in fact, in this area of decision-making that economic theories and tools of economic analysis make the greatest contribution in business.

If for instance, a business firm plans to launch a new product for which close substitutes are available in the market, one method of deciding whether or not this product should be launched is to obtain the services of a business consultant. The other method would be for the decision-maker or manager to decide. In doing this, the manager would need to investigate and analyse the following thoroughly:

(a) production related issues; and,
(b) sales prospects and problems.

With regards to production, the manager will be required to collect and analyse information or data on:

(c) available production techniques;
(d) cost of production associated with each production technique;
(e) supply position of inputs required for the production process;
(f) input prices;
(g) production costs of the competitive products; and,
(h) availability of foreign exchange, if inputs are to be imported.

Regarding the sales prospects and problems, the manager will be required to collect and analyse data on:

(a) general market trends;
(b) the industrial business trends;
(c) major existing and potential competitors, as well as their respective market shares;
(d) prices of the competing products;
(e) pricing strategies of the prospective competitors;
(f) market structure and the degree of competition; and,
(g) the supply position of complementary goods.

The application of economic theories in solving business problems helps in facilitating decision-making in the following ways:

First, it can give clear understanding of the various necessary economic concepts, including demand, supply, cost, price, and the like that are used in business analysis.

Second, it can help in ascertaining the relevant variables and specifying the relevant data. For example, in deciding what variables need to be considered in estimating the demand for two different sources of energy, petrol and electricity.

Third, it provides consistency to business analysis and helps in arriving at right conclusions.

3.3 Scope of Managerial Economics

Managerial economics comprises both micro- and macro-economic theories. Generally, the scope of managerial economics extends to those economic concepts, theories, and tools of analysis used in analysing the business environment, and to find solutions to practical business problems. In broad terms, managerial economics is applied economics.

The areas of business issues to which economic theories can be directly applied is divided into two broad categories:
1. Operational or internal issues; and,
2. Environment or external issues.

Operational problems are of internal nature. These problems include all those problems which arise within the business organization and fall within the control of management. Some of the basic internal issues include:
(f) choice of business and the nature of product (what to produce);
(g) choice of size of the firm (how much to produce);
(h) choice of technology (choosing the factor combination);
(i) choice of price (product pricing);
(j) how to promote sales;
(k) how to face price competition;
(l) how to decide on new investments;
(m) how to manage profit and capital; and,
(n) how to manage inventory.

The microeconomic theories dealing with most of these internal issues include, among others:
4. The ***theory of demand***, which explains the consumer behaviour in terms of decisions on whether or not to buy a commodity and the quantity to be purchased.
5. ***Theory of Production and production decisions***. The theory of production or theory of the firm explains the relationship between inputs and output.
6. ***Analysis of Market structure and Pricing theory***. Price theory explains how prices are determined under different market conditions.
7. ***Profit analysis and profit management***. Profit making is the most common business objective. However, making a satisfactory profit is not always

6

guaranteed due to business uncertainties. Profit theory guides firms in the measurement and management of profits, in making allowances for the risk premium, in calculating the pure return on capital and pure profit, and for future profit planning.
8. Theory of capital and investment decisions. Capital is the foundation of any business. It efficient allocation and management is one of the most important tasks of the managers, as well as the determinant of the firm's success level. Some of the important issues related to capital include: choice of investment project; assessing the efficiency of capital; and, the most efficient allocation of capital.

Environmental issues are issues related to the general business environment. These are issues related to the overall economic, social, and political atmosphere of the country in which the business is situated. The factors constituting *economic environment* of a country include:

1. The existing economic system
2. General trends in production, income, employment, prices, savings and investment, and so on.
3. Structure of the financial institutions.
4. Magnitude of and trends in foreign trade.
5. Trends in labour and capital markets.
6. Government's economic policies.
7. Social organizations, such as trade unions, consumers' cooperatives, and producer unions.
8. The political environment.
9. The degree of openness of the economy.

Managerial economics is particularly concerned with those economic factors that form the business climate. In macroeconomic terms, managerial economics focus on business cycles, economic growth, and content and logic of some relevant government activities and policies which form the business environment.

3.4 Managerial Economics and Gap between Theory and Practice

The Gap between Theory and Practice

It is a general knowledge that there exists a gap between theory and practice in the world of economic thinking and behaviour. By implication, a theory which appears logically sound might not be directly applicable in practice. Take for instance, when there are economies of scale, it seems theoretically sound that when inputs are doubled, output will be more or less doubled, and when inputs are tripled, output would be more or less tripled. This theoretical conclusion may not hold in practice.

Economic theories are highly simplistic because they are propounded on the basis of economic models based on simplifying assumptions. Through economic models, economists create a simplified world with its restrictive boundaries from which they derive their conclusions. Although economic models are said to be an extraction from the real world, the closeness of this extraction depends on how realistic the assumptions of the model are. It is a general belief that assumptions of economic models are unrealistic in most cases. The most common assumption of the economic models, as you may recall, is the *ceteris paribus* assumptions (that is all other things being constant or equal). This assumption has been alleged to be the most unrealistic assumption.

Though economic theories are, no doubt, hypothetical in nature, in their abstract form however, they do look divorced from reality. Abstract economic theories cannot be simply applied to real life situations. This however, does not mean that economic models and theories do not serve useful purposes. Microeconomic theory, for example, facilitates the understanding of what would be a complicated confusion of billions of facts by constructing simplified models of behaviour that are sufficiently similar to the actual phenomenon to be of help in understanding them. It cannot, nevertheless, be denied the fact that there is a gap between economic theory and practice. The gap arises from the fact that there exists a gap between the abstract world of economic models and the real world.

It suffices to say that although economic theories do not directly offer custom-made solutions to business problems, they provide a framework for logical economic thinking and analysis. The need for such a framework arises because the real economic world is too complex to permit consideration of every bit of economic facts that influence economic decisions. Economic analysis presents the business decision makers with a road map; it guides them to their destinations, and does not take them to their destinations.

Managerial economics can bridge the gap between economic theory and real world business decisions. The managerial economic logic and tools of analysis guide business decision makers in:
1. identifying their problems in the achievement
2. collecting the relevant data and related facts;
3. processing and analysing the facts;
4. drawing the relevant conclusions;
5. determining and evaluating the alternative means of achieving the goal; and,
6. taking a decision.

Without the application of economic logic and tools of analysis, business decisions may likely be irrational and arbitrary. Irrationality is highly counter-productive.

3.5 Self-Assessment Exercise
Discuss the important phases of business decision making processes

4.0 Conclusion

This unit has been able to expose you to what managerial economics is all about and why it is necessary to have it for effective business decisions. Managerial Economics comprises both micro-and macro-economic theories. Its scope extends to those economic concepts, theories, and tools of analysis used in the analysis of business environment, and to find solutions to practical business problems.

5.0 Summary

To put some light to the understanding and appreciation of managerial economics as a tool of business analysis, the unit focused on the following issues:

1. Economic analysis and business decisions, where it was pointed out that business decision-making basically involves the selection of best out of alternative opportunities open to the business enterprise.

2. Scope of Managerial Economics, where we learned that the scope of managerial economics extends to some economic concepts and tools used in analysing the business environment in order to seek for solutions to practical business problems.

3. Managerial Economics and the gap between theory and practice, where it was pointed out that there exists a gap between theory and practice in the world of economic thinking and behaviour. Managerial economics can bridge this gap through logic and tools of analysis that guide business decision makers.

6.0 Tutor-Marked Assignment

Why is the understanding of the principles of Managerial Economics necessary for a business manager?

7.0 References

Dwivedi, D. N. (2002) *Managerial Economics, sixth edition* (New Delhi: Vikas Publishing House Ltd).

UNIT 2: MEANING AND THEORIES OF PROFIT

Content
1.0 Introduction
2.0 Objectives
3.0 The Theory of Profit
3.1 Theories of Profit
3.2 Monopoly Profit
3.3 Self-Assessment Exercise
4.0 Conclusion
5.0 Summary
6.0 Tutor-Marked Assignment
7.0 References

1.0 Introduction

The term *profit* means different things to different people. Businesspeople, accountants, tax collectors, employees, and economists have their individual meaning of profit. In its general sense, profit is regarded as income accruing to equity holders, in the same sense as wages accrue to the workers; rent accrues to owners of rentable assets; and, interest accrues to the money lenders. To the accountant, 'profit' means the excess of revenue over all paid out costs, such as manufacturing and overhead expenses. It is more like what is referred to a 'net profit'. For practical purposes profit or business income refers to *profit* in accounting sense. Economist's concept of profit is the *pure profit* or 'economic profit'. Economic profit is a return over and above the *opportunity cost*, that is, the income expected from the second alternative investment or use of business resources. In this unit, emphasis will be placed on the various concepts of profit.

2.0 Objectives

By the time you must have gone through this unit, you will be able to:

1. Define profit and differentiate between Accounting profit and pure Economic profit.
2. Be familiar with the different theories of profit.
3. Understand what is meant by monopoly profit.

3.0 The Theories of Profit

Before exposing you to the theories of profit, it will be helpful for you to distinguish between two often misunderstood profit concepts: the Accounting profit and the Economic profit.

The Accounting Profit

Accounting profit may be defined as follows:

Accounting Profit = $\pi_a = TR - (w + r + I + m)$

where TR = Total Revenue; w = wages and salaries; r = rent; i = interest; and m = cost of materials.

You can observe that when calculating accounting profit, it is only the explicit or book costs that are considered and subtracted from the total revenue (TR).

The Economic or Pure Profit

Unlike accounting profit, economic profit takes into account both the explicit costs and implicit or imputed costs. The implicit or opportunity cost can be defined as the payment that would be necessary to draw forth the factors of production from their most remunerative alternative use or employment. *Opportunity cost* is the income is the income foregone which the business could expect from the second best alternative use of resources. The foregone incomes referred to here include interest, salary, and rent, often called *transfer costs.*

Economic profit also makes provision for (a) insurable risks, (b) depreciation, (c) necessary minimum payment to shareholders to prevent them from withdrawing their capital investments. Economic profit may therefore be defined as 'residual left after all contractual costs, including the
transfer costs of management, insurable risks, depreciation, and payments to shareholders have been met. Thus,

Economic or Pure Profit = $\pi_e = татTR - EC - IC$

where EC = Explicit Costs; and, IC = Implicit Costs.

Note that economic profit as defined by the above equation may necessarily not be positive. It may be negative since it may be difficult to decide beforehand the best way of using the business resources. Pure profit is a short-term phenomenon. It does not exist in the long-run under perfectly competitive conditions.

3.1 Theories of Profit
The unsettled controversy on the sources of profit has led to the emergence of various theories of profit in economics. The following discussions summarise the main theories.

3.1.1 Walker's Theory of Profit: Profit as Rent of Ability
One of the widely known theories of profit was stated by F. A. Walker who theorised 'profit' as the rent of "exceptional abilities that an entrepreneur may possess" over others. He believes that profit is the difference between the earnings of the least and the most efficient entrepreneurs. Walker assumes a state of perfect competition, in which all firms are presumed equal managerial ability. In Walker's view, under perfectly competitive

conditions, there would be no pure or economic profit and all firms would earn only marginal wages, which is popularly known in economics as *'normal profit'*.

3.1.2 Clark's Dynamic Theory
The J. B. Clark's theory is of the opinion that profits arise in a dynamic economy, not in a static economy. A static economy is defined as the one in which there is absolute freedom of competition; population and capital are stationary; production process remains unchanged over time; goods continue to remain homogeneous; there is freedom of factor mobility; there is no uncertainty and no risk; and if risk exists, it is insurable. In a static economy therefore, firms make only the 'normal profit' or the wages of management.

A dynamic economy on the other hand, is characterized by the following generic changes:
(i) population increases;
(ii) increase in capital;
(iii) improvement in production technique;
(iv) changes in the forms of business organizations; and,
(v) multiplication of consumer wants.

The major functions of entrepreneurs or managers in a dynamic environment are in taking advantage of the generic changes and promoting their businesses, expanding sales, and reducing costs. The entrepreneurs who successfully take advantage of changing conditions in a dynamic economy make pure profit.

From Clark's point of view, pure profit exist only in the short-run. In the long-run, competition forces other firms to imitate changes made by the leading firms, leading to a rise in demand for factors of production. Consequently, production costs rise, thus reducing profits, especially when revenue remains unchanged.

3.1.3 Hawley's Risk Theory of Profit
The risk theory of profit was initiated by F. B. Hawley in 1893. According to Hawley, risk in business may arise due to such reasons as obsolescence of a product, sudden fall in the market prices, non-availability of crucial raw materials, introduction of better substitutes by competitors, risk due to fire, war and the like. Risk taking is regarded as an inevitable accompaniment of dynamic production, and those who take risk have a sound claim of a separate reward, referred to as 'profit'. Hawley simply refers to profit as the price paid by society for assuming business risk. He suggests that businesspeople would not assume risk without expecting adequate compensation in excess of actuarial value, that is, premium on calculable risk.

3.1.4 Knight's Theory of Profit
Frank Knight treated profit as a residual return to uncertainty bearing, not to risk bearing as in the case of Hawley's. Knight divided risk into calculable and non-calculable risks. Calculable risks are those risks whose probability of occurrence can be statistically estimated on the basis of available data. Examples of these types of risks are risks due to

fire, theft, accidents, and the like. Calculable risks are insurable. Those areas of risk in which the probability of its occurrence is non-calculable, such as certain elements of production cost that cannot be accurately calculated, are not insurable.

3.1.5 Schumpeter's Innovation Theory of Profit
The innovation theory of profit was developed by Joseph A. Schumpeter. Schumpeter was of the opinion that factors such as emergence of interest and profits, recurrence of trade cycles are only incidental to a distinct process of economic development; and certain principles which could explain the process of economic development would also explain these economic variables or factors. Schumpeter's theory of profit is thus embedded in his theory of economic growth.

In his explanation of the process of economic growth, Schumpeter began with the state of stationary equilibrium, characterised by equilibrium in all spheres. Under conditions of stationary equilibrium, total receipts from the business are exactly equal to the total cost outlay, and there is no profit. According to the Schumpeter's theory, profit can be made only by introducing innovations in manufacturing technique, as well as in the methods of supplying the goods. Sources of innovation include:
1. Introduction of new commodity or a better quality good;
2. Introduction of new method of production;
3. Opening of a new market;
4. Discovery of new sources of raw material; and,
5. Organising the industry in an innovative manner with the new techniques.

3.2 Monopoly Profit
Observe that the profit theories presented above were propounded in the background of the existence of perfect competition. But as conceived in the theoretical models, perfect competition is either non-existent or is a rare phenomenon. An extreme opposite of perfect competition is the existence of monopoly in the market. The term monopoly characterises a market situation in which there is a single seller of a commodity that does not have close substitutes.

Monopoly arises due to such factors as:
(i) economies of scale;
(ii) sole ownership;
(iii) legal sanction and protection; and,
(iv) mergers and acquisition.

A monopolist can earn pure or 'monopoly' profit and maintain it in the long run by using its monopoly powers, including:
(i) powers to control price and supply;
(ii) powers to prevent entry of competitors by price cutting; and,
(iii) monopoly power in certain input markets.

3.3 Self-Assessment Exercise

Discuss the basic difference between accounting profit and economic profit. In your personal opinion, which of the different theories of profit you learned from this unit do you think is more businesslike and why?

4.0 Conclusion

This unit has presented another important aspect in the understanding and application of managerial economics: the meaning and theories of profit. Though it was observed that profit means different things to different people, you should bear in mind that, for practical purposes, profit or business income refers to profit in accounting sense. The Economist's concept of profit is the pure profit defined as a return over and above the opportunity cost.

There are several important theories of profit among which are: the Walker's theory; the Clark's dynamic theory; Hawley's theory; Knight's theory; and, the Schumpeter's Innovation theory.

5.0 Summary

This unit serves as an important background to the study of managerial economics. It has presented the basic definitions of profit, both in business accounting and economic terms. In accounting terms, profit has been defined simply as the difference between revenue from sales and explicit or out-of-pocket costs. In economic terms, profit was defined as the return over and above the opportunity costs, that is, the income expected from the second alternative investment or use of business resources. Economic profit makes provision for insurable risks, depreciation, necessary minimum payment to shareholders to prevent them from withdrawing their capital investments. It is also defined as 'the residual left after all contractual costs, including transfer costs of management, insurable risks, depreciation, and payments to shareholders have been met.

The discussions on the theory of profits have exposed you to the different important theories of profit, including: the Walker's theory which refers to profit as rent of ability; the Clark's dynamic theory which assumes that profits arise in a dynamic economy, not in a static economy; the Hawley's risk theory, which refers to profit as the price paid by society for assuming business risk; the Knight's theory which looks at profit as a residual return to uncertainty bearing, not to risk bearing as in Hawley's theory; and, Schumpeter's innovation theory, which is embedded in his theory of economic growth. Schumpeter believes that profit can only be made by introducing innovations in manufacturing techniques, as well as in the methods of supplying the goods produced.

6.0 Tutor-Marked Assignment

Enumerate the major areas of business decision making in business. Outline the reason it might be important to distinguish between accounting profit and economic or pure profit.

7.0 References

Dwivedi, D. N. (2002) *Managerial Economics, sixth edition* (New Delhi: Vikas Publishing House Ltd).

UNIT 3: PROFIT MAXIMISATION AS A BUSINESS OBJECTIVE

Content
1.0 Introduction
2.0 Objectives
3.0 Profit Maximisation Objective
3.1 The Profit-Maximising Conditions
3.2 Self-Assessment Exercise
4.0 Conclusion
5.0 Summary
6.0 Tutor-Marked Assignment
7.0 References

1.0 Introduction
The conventional economic theory assumes that profit maximisation is the only objective of business firms. Profit maximisation forms the basis of conventional price theory. It is the most reasonable, analytical, and 'productive' business objective. This unit begins by familiarizing you with the necessary and sufficient conditions for profit maximisation, followed by in depth presentations and business examples.

2.0 Objectives
At the end of this unit, you will be expected to:
1. Understand the reason a firm sets its objective to be that of profit maximisation
2. Know the necessary and sufficient conditions for profit maximisation.
3. Solve problems involving profit maximisation.

3.0 Profit Maximisation Objective
Profit maximisation objective helps in predicting the behaviour of business firms in the real world, as well as in predicting the behaviour of price and output under different market conditions. There are some theoretical profit-maximising conditions that we must have in our finger tips. These are presented below:

3.1 The Profit-Maximising Conditions
We first define profit as:

$$= TR - TC, \qquad (3.1.1)$$

where TR = Total Revenue = Unit price (P) x Quantity (Q) = PQ, and,

TC = Total cost = Variable Cost (VC) + Fixed Cost (FC).

There are two major conditions that must be fulfilled for equation (3.1.1) to be a maximum profit: (i) the first-order (or necessary) condition, and (ii) the second-order (or supplementary) condition.

The *first-order condition* requires that at a maximum profit, marginal revenue (MR) must equal marginal Cost (MC). Note that by the term 'marginal revenue', we mean the revenue obtained from the production and sale of one additional unit of output, while 'marginal cost' is the cost arising from the production of the one additional unit of output.

The **second-order condition** requires that the first-order condition must be satisfied under the condition of decreasing marginal revenue (MR) and increasing marginal cost (MC). Fulfillment of this two conditions makes the second-order condition the *sufficient condition* for profit maximizations.

The first-and second-order conditions can be illustrated as in figure 3.1 below:

Figure 3.1: Marginal Conditions of Profit Maximisation

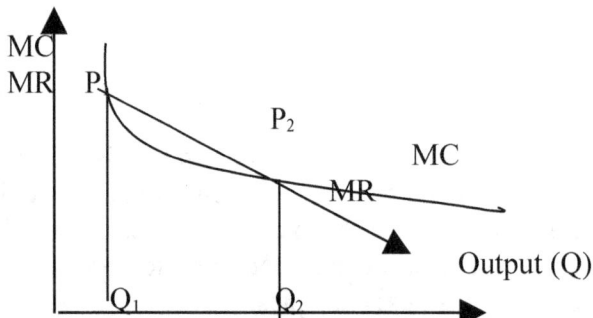

As you can see in figure 3.1, the first-order condition is satisfied at points P_1 and P_2, where MR = MC. But the second-order condition is satisfied only at point P_2, where technically, the second derivative of the profit function is negative. By implication, at this point, the total profit curve has turned downward after having reached its peak.

In technical terms, the profit-maximising conditions can be formulated as follows:
Given profit ( ) = TR – TC to be maximized, let:

TR = f(Q) and,
TC = f(Q)
where Q = quantity produced and sold.

Then = F(Q) = f(Q)$_{TR}$ – f(Q)$_{TC}$ (3.1.2)

The first-order condition requires that the first derivative of equation (3.1.2) should be zero, so that:

$$\frac{d}{dQ} = \frac{dTR}{dQ} - \frac{dTC}{dQ} = 0 \qquad (3.1.3)$$

You can observe that this condition holds only when:

$$\frac{dTR}{dQ} = \frac{dTC}{dQ}$$

or

MR = MC.

To get the second-order condition, we take the second derivative of the profit function to get:

$$\frac{d^2\pi}{dQ^2} = \frac{d^2TR}{dQ^2} - \frac{d^2TC}{dQ^2} \qquad (3.1.4)$$

The second-order condition requires that equation (3.1.4) is negative, so that:

$$\frac{d^2TR}{dQ^2} - \frac{d^2TC}{dQ^2} < 0$$

or

$$\frac{d^2TR}{dQ^2} < \frac{d^2TC}{dQ^2} \qquad (3.1.5)$$

Equation (3.1.5) may also be written as:

Slope of MR < Slope of MC,

since the left-hand side of equation (3.1.5) represents the slope of MR and the right-hand side represents the slope of MC.

This implies that at the optimum point of profit maximisation, marginal cost (MC) must intersect the marginal revenue (MR) from below.

We conclude that maximum profit occurs where the first- and second-order conditions are satisfied.

Example

Suppose that the unit price of a commodity is defined by:
$$P = 100 - 2Q \qquad (3.1.6)$$
Then, $TR = PQ = (100 - 2Q) Q$
$$= 100Q - 2Q^2 \qquad (3.1.7)$$

Suppose also that the total cost of producing this commodity is defined by the cost function:
$$TC = 100 + 0.5Q^2 \qquad (3.1.8)$$
You are required to apply the first-order condition for profit maximisation and determine the profit-maximising level of output.

According to the first-order condition, profit is maximized where:

MR = MC,

Or

$$\frac{dTR}{dQ} = \frac{dTC}{dQ}$$

Given equations (3.1.7) and (3.1.8), we get:

$$MR = \frac{dTR}{dQ} = 100 - 4Q \qquad (3.1.9)$$

$$MC = \frac{dTC}{dQ} = 1Q = Q \qquad (3.1.10)$$

It follows that profit is maximized where:
MR = MC

Or

$$100 - 4Q = Q \qquad (3.1.11)$$

Solving for Q in equation (3.1.11), we get:

100 = 5Q
5Q = 100
Q = 100/5 = 20.

The output level of 20 units satisfies the first-order condition. Let us see if it satisfies the second-order condition.

Recall that the second-order condition requires that:

$$\frac{d^2TR}{dQ^2} - \frac{d^2TC}{dQ^2} < 0$$

or

$$\frac{dMR}{dQ} - \frac{dMC}{dQ} < 0$$

or

$$\frac{d(100 - 4Q)}{dQ} - \frac{d(Q)}{dQ} < 0$$

-4 -1 = -5 < 0

Thus the second-order condition is also satisfied at the output level of 20 units. We therefore conclude that the profit-maximising level of output in this problem is 20 units.

To determine the maximum profit, you will substitute 20 for Q in the original profit function. Thus, the maximum profit will be:

$* = TR - TC$

$= 100Q - 2Q^2 - (10 + 0.5Q^2)$

$= 100Q - 2.5Q^2 - 10$

$= 100(20) - 2.5(20)^2 - 10$

$= 2000 - 1000 - 10$

$= 990.$

We conclude that the maximum profit is N990 only.

3.2 Self-Assessment Exercise
Examine critically profit maximisation as the objective of business firms and discuss the alternative objectives of business firms.

4.0 Conclusion
Profit maximisation has been the prime objective of classical business organizations. To maximise profit, certain conditions must be met, the first being that at optimum profit-maximising point, the firm's marginal revenue must equal marginal cost. Second, to ensure that maximum profit is attained, the second derivative of the profit function is expected to be less than zero.

5.0 Summary
This unit informs you that profit maximisation objective helps in predicting the behaviour of business firms in the real world, as well as in predicting the behaviour of price and output under different market conditions. In the discussions, you noted that profit can basically be defined as the difference between revenue and costs. To maximize profit, marginal revenue is equated with marginal cost. We refer to this as the first-order condition. The second-order condition requires that the first-order condition must be satisfied under the condition of decreasing marginal revenue (MR) and increasing marginal cost (MC).

6.0 Tutor-Marked Assignment
Assuming the unit price of a commodity is defined by: $P = 90 - 2q$, and the cost function is given as: $C = 10 + 0.5 q^2$,
1. Determine the profit-maximising level of output and the unit price.

2. Determine the cost-minimising level of output

7.0 References
1. Dwivedi, D. N. (2002) ***Managerial Economics, sixth edition*** (New Delhi: Vikas Publishing House Ltd).

2. Haessuler, E. F. and Paul, R. S. (1976), ***Introductory Mathematical Analysis for Students of Business and Economics, 2nd edition*** (Reston Virginia: Reston Publishing Company)

UNIT 4: OTHER BUSINESS OBJECTIVES

Content
1.0 Introduction
2.0 Objectives
3.0 Other Relevant Business Objectives
3.1 Sales, Growth Rate, and Maximisation of Utility Function as
    Business Objectives
3.2 Self-Assessment Exercise
4.0 Conclusion
5.0 Summary
6.0 Tutor-Marked Assignment
7.0 References

1.0 Introduction
Apart from profit maximisation, as you all know, business firms have the following objectives:
1. Maximisation of Sales revenue
2. Maximisation of the growth rate
3. Maximisation of manager's utility function
4. Making satisfactory rate of profit
5. Long-run survival of the firm
6. Entry-prevention and risk-avoidance.

In this unit, we discuss these other business objectives with the aim of acquainting you with the several reasons an entrepreneur will choose to be in business.

2.0 Objectives
Having gone through this unit, you will be able to:
1. Be more informed on objectives of a business organisation
2. Know the techniques of maximising revenue, output, and minimising costs
3. Be able to make effective decisions for business expansion and growth.

3.0 Other Relevant Business Objectives
**3.1 Sales, Growth Rate, and Maximisation of Utility Function as
    Business Objectives**

3.1.1 Sales Revenue Maximisation as Business Objective
It was one famous economist, W. J. Baumol, who introduced the hypothesis of Sales Revenue maximisation as an alternative to the profit-maximisation objective. Baumol's reason for the introduction of this hypothesis is the usual dichotomy between business ownership and management, especially in large corporations. This dichotomy, according to Baumol, gives managers some opportunity to set their personal goals other than profit maximisation goal which business owners pursue. Given the opportunity, managers would want to maximise their own utility function. And, the most plausible factor in managers' utility functions is the maximisation of sales revenue. Baumol lists the factors that explain the managers' pursuance of this goal as follows:

First, salary and other monetary benefits of managers tend to be more closely related to sales revenue than to profits.

Second, banks and other financial institutions look at sales revenue while financing business ventures.

Third, trend in sales revenue is a readily available indicator of a firm's performance.

Fourth, increasing sales revenue enhances manager's prestige while profits go to the business owners.

Fifth, managers find profit maximisation a difficult objective to fulfill consistently over time and at the same level. Profits fluctuate with changing economic conditions.

Finally, growing sales tend to strengthen competitive spirit of the firm in the market, and *vice versa*.

3.1.2 Technique of Total Revenue Maximisation

As noted earlier, total revenue (TR) can be defined by

$$TR = PQ \tag{3.1.1}$$

where P refers to unit price and Q refers to quantity sold.

The optimisation problem here is to find the value of Q that maximises total revenue.

The rule for maximising total revenue is that total revenue will be maximized at the level of sales (Q) for which marginal (MR) = 0. In other words, the revenue from the sale of the marginal unit of the product must be equal to zero at the point of maximum revenue.

The marginal revenue (MR) is the first derivative of the total revenue (TR) function. For example, we want to find the level of Q for which revenue will be maximized if the price function is given by:

$$P = 500 - 5Q \tag{3.1.2}$$

Then by equation (3.1.1),

$$TR = PQ = (500 - 5Q)Q$$

$$= 500Q - 5Q^2 \tag{3.1.3}$$

$$\text{Marginal revenue (MR)} = \frac{dTR}{dQ} = 500 - 10Q \tag{3.1.4}$$

Setting equation (3.1.4) equal to zero according to the rule, we get:

500 − 10Q = 0   (3.1.5)

solving for Q in equation (3.1.5), we get:

500 = 10Q

or, 10 Q = 500

     Q = 50.

This indicates that the revenue-maximising level of output is 50 units.

The maximum total revenue can be obtained by substituting 50 for Q in the total revenue function,

$TR = 500Q - 5Q^2$

Thus, $TR = 500(50) - 5(50)^2$

         = 25,000 − 12,500

         = N12,500.

3.1.3 Technique of Output Maximisation: Minimisation of Average Cost

The optimum size of the firm is the size minimises the average cost of production. This is also referred to as the most efficient size of the firm. Knowledge of the optimum size of a firm is very important for future planning under three important conditions:

First, a businessperson planning to set up a new production unit would like to know the optimum size of the plant for future planning. This issue arises because, as the theory of production indicates, the average cost of production in most productive activities decreases to a certain level of output and then begins to increase.

Second, the firms planning to expand their scale of production would like to know the most efficient level of the economies of scale so that they can be able to plan the marketing of the product accordingly.

Third, businesspeople working under competitive business environment are faced with a given market price. Their profit therefore, depends on their ability to reduce their unit cost of production. And, given the technology and input prices, the prospect of reducing unit cost of production depends on the size of production. The problem decision makers face under this condition is how to find the optimum level of output or the level of output that minimises the average cost of production.

As implied earlier, under general production conditions, the optimum level of output is the one that minimises the average cost (AC), where the average cost can be defined as the ratio between total cost (TC) and quantity produced (Q). Thus,

$$AC = \frac{TC}{Q} \quad (3.1.6)$$

Suppose the total cost function of a firm is given by:

$$TC = 100 + 60Q + 4Q^2 \quad (3.1.7)$$

then,

$$AC = \frac{TC}{Q} = \frac{100+60Q+4Q^2}{Q}$$

$$= \frac{100}{Q} + 60 + 4Q \quad (3.1.8)$$

The problem here is to find the value of Q that minimises the average cost, as represented in equation (3.1.8).

The *Minimisation Rule.* Like the maximisation rule, the minimization rule is that the derivative of the function to be minimised must be equal to zero. It follows that the value the value of output (Q) that minimises average cost (AC) can be obtained by taking the first derivative of the AC function and setting it equal to zero and solving for Q.

Thus, in the current example,

$$\frac{dAC}{dQ} = \frac{d(100Q^{-1} + 60 + 4Q)}{dQ} = \frac{-100}{Q^2} + 4 \quad (3.1.9)$$

Setting equation (2.3.9) equal to zero, we get:

$-100/Q^2 + 4 = 0$

$-100/Q^2 = -4$

$-4Q^2 = -100$

$Q^2 = 100/4 = 25$

$Q = \sqrt{25} = 5$

Thus, the level of output that minimises average cost is 5 units.

3.1.4 Maximisation of Firm's Growth Rate as an Alternative Objective

According to Robin Marris, managers attempt to maximise a firm's *balanced growth rate*, subject to managerial and financial constraints. Marris defines firm's balanced growth rate (G) as:

$$G = G_D = G_C \qquad (3.1.20)$$

where G_D and G_C are growth rate of demand for the firm's product and growth rate of capital supply to the firm, respectively.

Simply stated, a firm's growth rate is said to be balanced when demand for its product and supply of capital to the firm increase at the same rate. Marris translated these two growth rates into two utility functions: (i) manager's utility function (U_m), and (ii) business owner's utility function (U_o), where:

$$U_m = f(\text{salary, power, job security, prestige, status}). \qquad (3.1.21)$$

$$U_o = f(\text{output, capital, market-share, profit, public esteem}). \qquad (3.1.22)$$

The maximisation of business owner's utility (U_o) implies maximisation of demand for the firm's product or growth of the supply of capital.

3.1.5 Maximisation of Managerial Utility Function as an Alternative Objective

O. E. Williamson propounded the hypothesis of maximisation of managerial utility function. He argues that managers have the freedom to pursue objectives other than profit maximisation. Managers seek to maximise their own utility function subject to a minimum level of profit. According to Williamson, manager's utility function can be expressed as:

$$U = f(S, M, I_D) \qquad (3.1.23)$$

where S = additional expenditure on staff
M = managerial emoluments
I_D = discretionary investments

According to the hypothesis, managers attempt to maximise their utility function subject to a satisfactory profit. A minimum profit is necessary to satisfy the shareholders or else the manager's job security will be at stake.

3.1.6 Long-run Survival and Market-share as a Business Objective

K. W. Rothschild proposed the hypothesis of long-run survival and market-share goals. According to the hypothesis, the primary goal of the firm is long-run survival. Other economists suggest that attainment and retention of a constant market share is an additional objective of the firms. Managers therefore, seek to secure their market share and long-run survival. The firms may seek to maximise their long-run profit, which may not be certain.

3.1.7 Entry-prevention and Risk-avoidance as Business Objective

Other alternative objectives of business firms as suggested by economists are the prevention of entry of new firms and risk avoidance. It is argued that the motive behind entry-prevention may be any or all of the followings:

(a) profit maximisation in the long-run;
(b) securing a constant market share; and,
(c) avoidance of risk caused by unpredictable behaviour of new firms.

The advocates of profit maximisation as business objective argue, however, that only profit-maximising firms can survive in the long-run. Firms can achieve all other subsidiary objectives and goals easily only if they can maximise their profits.
Another argument is that prevention of entry may be the major objective in the pricing policy of the firm, particularly in the case of limit pricing. But the motive behind entry-prevention is to secure a constant share in the market, which is compatible with profit maximisation.

3.2 Self-Assessment Exercise

Outline the major reasons a manager must know the objectives of a business firm, apart from profit maximisation.

4. Conclusion

We have discovered from this unit that, apart from profit maximisation, business firms have the following objectives:
Maximisation of Sales revenue
Maximisation of the growth rate
Maximisation of manager's utility function
Making satisfactory rate of profit
Long-run survival of the firm
Entry-prevention and risk-avoidance.

The advocates of profit maximisation as business objective argue, however, that firms can achieve all other subsidiary objectives and goals easily only if they can maximise their profits.
Another important argument has been that prevention of entry may be the major objective in the pricing policy of the firm, particularly in the case of limit pricing. But the motive behind entry-prevention is to secure a constant share in the market, which is compatible with profit maximisation.

5.0 Summary

This unit stress the point that managers often set their personal goals different from profit maximisation, the goal usually pursued by business owners. Some good examples of such manager objectives are sales, growth rate, and maximisation of utility function. The factors explaining this include the fact that:

First, salary and other monetary benefits of managers tend to be more closely related to sales revenue than to profits.

Second, banks and other financial institutions look at sales revenue while financing business ventures.

Third, trend in sales revenue is a readily available indicator of a firm's performance.

Fourth, increasing sales revenue enhances manager's prestige while profits go to the business owners.

Fifth, managers find profit maximisation a difficult objective to fulfill consistently over time and at the same level. Profits fluctuate with changing economic conditions.

Finally, growing sales tend to strengthen competitive spirit of the firm in the market, and *vice versa.*

Other similar objectives include: making satisfactory profit rate, long-run survival of the firm, and entry-prevention and risk-avoidance. Knowledge of these other business objectives is essential for management decisions.

6. Tutor-Marked Assignments
Apart from the business objectives discussed in this unit, can you enumerate and discuss briefly other business objectives you can think of?

7. References
Dwivedi, D. N. (2002) *Managerial Economics, sixth edition* (New Delhi: Vikas Publishing House Ltd).

UNIT 5: CONTRAINED OPTIMISATION

Content
1.0 Introduction
2.0 Objectives
3.0 The Constrained Optimisation Techniques

3.1 Constrained Optimisation by Substitution Method
3.2 Constrained Optimisation by Lagrangian Multiplier Method
3.3 Self-Assessment Exercise
4.0 Conclusion
5.0 Summary
6.0 Tutor-Marked Assignment
7.0 References

1.0 Introduction

The maximisation and minimization techniques as referred to and discussed in the previous units are generally referred to in economics as *unconstrained* optimisation or minimisation, as the case may be. They are unconstrained in the sense that firms are assumed to operate under no constraints on their activities. In the real business world however, firms face serious resource constraints. They need, for example, to maximise output with given quantity of capital and labour time. The techniques used to optimise the business objective(s) under constraints are referred to as *constrained optimisation techniques.* The three common techniques of optimisation include: *(i) Linear Programming, (ii) constrained optimisation by substitution,* and
(iii) Lagrangian multiplier. The linear programming technique has a wide range of applications and should be a subject in itself, usually discussed in detail under quantitative techniques in economics. This discussion will attempt to summarise the two other important techniques, that is, constrained optimisation by substitution and Lagrangian multiplier.

2.0 Objectives

At the end of this unit, you will be expected to:

1. Understand the meaning and importance of constrained optimisation
2. Know the applicable techniques in constrained optimisation
3. be able to apply optimisation principles in business decisions

3.0 The Constrained Optimisation Techniques

There are basically two mostly used optimisation techniques including: the substitution method; and, the Lagrangian multiplier method

3.1 Constrained Optimisation by Substitution Method

This technique will be illustrated in two ways: (i) constrained profit maximisation problem, and (ii) constrained cost minimisation problems.

3.1.1 Constrained Profit Maximisation

Let the profit function of an hypothetical firm be given as:

$$= f(X, Y) = 100X - 2X^2 - XY + 180Y - 4Y^2 \qquad (3.1.1)$$

Where X and Y represent two products.

We wish to maximise equation (3.1.1) subject to the constraint that the sum of the output of X and Y be equal to 30 units. That is,

X + Y = 30 (3.1.2)

Solving by the substitution method, we obtain as follows:

First note that the process of the substitution method involves two steps
1. express one of the variables (X or Y in this case) in terms of the other and solve the constraint equation for one of them (X or Y), and
2. substitute the solution obtained into the objective function (that is, the function to be maximized or the profit function) and solve the outcome for the other variable.

Solution

Given the constraint equation 3.1.2), we solve for the values of X and Y in terms of one another to obtain:

X = 30 − Y

Or

Y = 30 − X

By substituting the value of X into the profit equation (3.1.1), we obtain:

$$\begin{aligned}
&= 100(30 - Y) - 2(30 - Y)^2 - (30 - Y)Y + 180Y - 4Y^2 \\
&= 3000 - 100Y - 2(900 - 60Y + Y^2) - 30Y + Y^2 + 180Y - 4Y^2 \\
&= 3000 - 100Y - 1800 + 120Y - 2Y^2 - 30Y + Y^2 + 180Y - 4Y^2 \\
&= 1200 + 170Y - 5Y^2
\end{aligned}$$
(3.1.3)

Equation (3.1.3) can now be maximised by obtaining the first derivative and setting it equal to zero and solving for Y:

$$\frac{d}{dY} = 170 - 10Y = 0 \qquad (3.1.4)$$

Solving equation (3.1.4) for Y, we get:

10Y = 170

Y = 17.

Substituting 17 for Y into the constraint equation (3.1.2), we get:

X + 17 = 30

X = 13

It follows that the optimum solution for the constrained profit maximisation problem is X = 13 units and Y = 17 units. This values of X and Y satisfy the constraint. Expressed differently, the firm maximises profit by producing and selling 13 units of product X and 17 units of product Y.

The maximum profit under the given constraint can now be obtained by substituting the above values of X and Y into the profit function, equation (3.1.1):

$$(X, Y) = (13, 17) = 100(13) - 2(13)^2 - (13)(17) + 180(17) - 4(17)^2$$
$$= 2,645.$$

Thus, the maximum profit under constraint is N2,645. It can be shown that maximum profits under constraints is less than maximum profits without constraints.

3.1.2 Constrained Cost Minimisation

We now apply the substitution method to the problem of constrained cost minimisation. Suppose the cost function of a firm producing two goods, X and Y, is given by:

$$C = 2X^2 - XY + 3Y^2$$

and the firm must meet a combined order of 36 units of the two goods. The problem is to find and optimum combination of the products X and Y that minimises the cost of production. Alternatively stated, we

Minimise $\quad C = 2X^2 - XY + 3Y^2 \quad\quad\quad\quad\quad\quad\quad\quad$ (3.1.5)

Subject to $\quad X + Y = 36 \quad\quad\quad\quad\quad\quad\quad\quad\quad\quad\quad\quad$ (3.1.6)

Again, substitution method requires that the constraint equation (3.1.6) is expressed in terms of any of the two goods, X and Y, and then substituted into the *objective function* (equation (3.1.5)). Expressing X in terms of Y, we get:

$$X = 36 - Y \quad\quad\quad\quad\quad\quad\quad\quad\quad\quad\quad\quad\quad\quad (3.1.7)$$

Substituting equation (3.1.7) for X in the objective function, you get:

$$C = 2(36 - Y)^2 - (36 - Y)Y + 3Y^2$$
$$= 2(1296 - 72Y + Y^2) - 36Y + Y^2 + 3Y^2$$
$$= 2592 - 144Y + 2Y^2 - 36Y + Y^2 + 3Y^2$$
$$= 2592 - 180Y + 6Y^2 \quad\quad\quad\quad\quad\quad\quad\quad (3.1.8)$$

According to the optimisation rule, for the now objective function (equation (3.1.8)) to be minimised, the first derivative must be equal to zero, viz:

$$\frac{dC}{dY} = 180 + 12Y = 0 \qquad (3.1.9)$$

Solving for Y in equation (3.1.9), we get the value of Y as follows:

$12Y = 180$
$Y = 15$

Substituting this value into the constraint equation (3.1.6), you get:
$X + 15 = 36$
$X = 21$

Thus, the optimum solution demands that 21 units of X and 15 units of Y minimise the cost of meeting the combined order of 36 units (that is, $21 + 15 = 36$ units). The minimum cost of producing 21 units of X and 15 units of Y can be obtained as follows, using equation (3.1.5), the objective function:

Minimum Cost $= 2X^2 - XY + 3Y^2$

$= 2(21)^2 - (21)(15) + 3(15)^2$

$= 882 - 315 + 675$

$= 1,242$

Thus, the minimum cost of producing the combined order is N1,242.

3.2 Constrained Optimisation by Lagrangian Multiplier Method
The lagrangian method is most useful in solving complex optimisation problems. In this discussion, we summarise this method using two illustrations:
5. a constrained profit maximisation problem, and
6. a constrained cost minimisation problem

3.2.1 Constrained Profit Maximisation
We refer to the profit function of equation (3.1.1), with some constraint imposed, so that we:

Maximse $\quad (X, Y) = 100X - 2X^2 - XY + 180Y - 4Y^2 \qquad (3.2.1)$

Subject to $\quad X + Y = 30 \qquad (3.2.2)$

The basic approach of the Lagrangian method is to combine the objective function and the constraint equation to form a Lagrangian function. This is then solved using partial first-order derivatives.

The Lagrangian function is formulated simply by:
First, setting the constraint equation (3.2.2) equal to zero:

$X + Y - 30 = 0$

Second, multiplying the resulting equation by λ (Greek letter, "lambda"):

$\lambda(X + Y - 30)$.

Adding this to the objective function, we get the Lagrangian function as:

$$Z = 100X - 2X^2 - XY + 180Y - 4Y^2 + \lambda(X + Y - 30) \qquad (3.2.3)$$

Equation (3.2.3) is the Lagrangian function with three unknowns, X, Y, and λ. The values of these unknowns that maximise Z will also maximize Profit (π). The Greek letter, λ, is referred to as the Lagrangian multiplier. It measures the impact of a small change in the constraint on the objective functions.

We are now required to maximise Z (equation (3.2.3). To do this, we first obtain the partial derivatives of Z with respect to X, Y, and λ and set each equal to zero to satisfy the first-order condition for optimisation. This will give rise to a simultaneous equation system in three unknowns, X, Y, and λ as indicated below:

$$Z = 100X - 2X^2 - XY + 180Y - 4Y^2 + \lambda(X + Y - 30)$$

$$\frac{\partial Z}{\partial X} = 100 - 4X - Y + \lambda = 0 \qquad (3.2.4)$$

$$\frac{\partial Z}{\partial Y} = -X + 180 - 8Y + \lambda = 0 \qquad (3.2.5)$$

$$\frac{\partial Z}{\partial \lambda} = X + Y - 30 = 0 \qquad (3.2.6)$$

Solving for X, Y, and λ in the above simultaneous equation system, you obtain the values of X, Y, and λ that maximise the objective function in equation (3.2.1). Using the necessary technique of solving simultaneous equation systems, you obtain the solutions:
X = 13
Y = 17, and,
λ = 31.

The value of λ implies that if output is increased by 1 unit, that is, from 30 to 31 units, profit will increase by about N31, and if output is decreased from 30 to 29 units, profit will decrease by about N31.

3.2.2 Constrained Cost Minimisation

Suppose a firm has to supply a combined order of 500 units of products X and Y. The joint cost function for the two products is given by:

$$C = 100X^2 + 150Y^2 \qquad (3.2.7)$$

Since the quantities to be produced of X and Y are not specified in the order, the firm is free to supply X and Y in any combination. The problem is therefore, to find the combination of X and Y that minimises cost of production, subject to the constraint, $X + Y = 500$. Thus, we are required to:

Minimise $\qquad C = 100X^2 + 150Y^2$

Subject to $\qquad X + Y = 500 \qquad (3.2.8)$

The Lagrangian function can be formulated as in equation (3.2.9) below:

$$Z_c = 100X^2 + 150Y^2 + \lambda(500 - X - Y) \qquad (3.2.9)$$

As before, the first-order partial derivatives yield:

$$\frac{\partial Z_c}{\partial X} = 200X - \lambda = 0 \qquad (3.2.10)$$

$$\frac{\partial Z_c}{\partial Y} = 300Y - \lambda = 0 \qquad (3.2.11)$$

$$\frac{\partial Z_c}{\partial \lambda} = 500 - X - Y = 0 \qquad (3.2.12)$$

Again, solving the above simultaneous equations for X, Y, and λ, we get the solution to the cost minimisation problem.

For simplicity, substract equation (3.2.11) from equation (3.2.10), you get:

$200X - \lambda - (300Y - \lambda) = 0$

$200X - 300Y = 0$

$200X = 300Y$

$\qquad X = 1.5Y \qquad (3.2.13)$

Substituting 1.5Y for X in equation (3.2.12), we get:

$500 - 1.5Y - Y = 0$

$500 - 2.5Y = 0$

$2.5Y = 500$

$Y = 200$

Substituting Y = 200 into the constraint equation (3.2.8), you get:

$X + 200 = 500$

$X = 300.$

It follows that the solution to the minimisation problem is that X = 300 and Y = 200 will minimise the cost of producing the combined 500 units of the products X and Y.

The minimum cost is obtained by using the objective function (equation (3.2.7)) as follows:

$C = 100X^2 + 150Y^2$

$= 100(300)^2 + 150(200)^2$

$= 9,000,000 + 6,000,000$

$= 15,000,000$

Thus the minimum cost of supplying the combined 500 units of products X and Y is N15 million.

3.3 Self-Assessment Exercise
Briefly discuss what you understand by constrained optimisation. How would you interpret the lagrangian multiplier.

4.0 Conclusion
This unit has presented the basic principles of constrained optimisation, with special emphasis on profit maximisation and cost minimisation. Among the various techniques of constrained optimisation, the ones that are used most of the time are: (i) the substitution method; and, (ii) the Lagrangian multiplier method.

5.0 Summary
The techniques used to optimise the business objective(s) under constraints are referred to as *constrained optimisation techniques.* The three common techniques of optimisation include: *(i) Linear Programming, (ii) constrained optimisation by substitution,* and *(iii) Lagrangian multiplier.* The linear programming technique has a wide range of applications and should be a subject in itself, usually discussed in detail under

quantitative techniques in economics. This unit has attempted to outline the two other important techniques, that is, constrained optimisation by substitution and Lagrangian multiplier. Both techniques were illustrated by profit maximisation and cost minimisation problems. Under the Langrangian method, a very important multiplier, the Langrangian multiplier, λ, was introduced. The value of λ would imply that if a business firm increases output by 1 unit, all things being equal, profit will increase by N1, and vice versa.

6.0 Tutor-Marked Assignment
The B-Products Plc produces two products, X and Y. The profit function of this company is given by:

$$= 10X - X^2 - XY + 18Y - 2Y^2$$

The company is under the obligation to produce a minimum combined output of 40 units. Find the number of units that will be produced of
the products X and Y, subject to the total of 40 units, that maximises
profit. Use the Lagrangian multiplier method.

7.0 References
1. Dwivedi, D. N. (2002) *Managerial Economics, sixth edition* (New Delhi: Vikas Publishing House Ltd).

2. Haessuler, E. F. and Paul, R. S. (1976), *Introductory Mathematical Analysis for Students of Business and Economics, 2nd edition* (Reston Virginia: Reston Publishing Company)

UNIT 6: DECISION ANALYSIS

Content
1.0 Introduction
2.0 Objectives
3.0 Decision Analysis

3.1 Certainty and Uncertainty in Decision Analysis
3.2 Analysis of the Decision Problem
3.3 Self-Assessment Exercise
4.0 Conclusion
5.0 Summary
6.0 Tutor-Marked Assignment
7.0 References

1.0 Introduction
Decision analysis is the modern approach to decision making both in economics and in business. It can be defined as the logical and quantitative analysis of all the factors influencing a decision. The analysis forces decision makers to assume some active roles in the decision-making process. By so doing, they rely more on rules that are consistent with their logic and personal behaviour than on the mechanical use of a set of formulas and tabulated probabilities.

The primary aim of decision analysis is to increase the likelihood of good outcomes by making good and effective decisions. A good decision must be consistent with the information and preferences of the decision maker. It follows that decision analysis provides decision-making framework based on available information on the business environment, be it a sample information, judgmental information, or a combination of both.

As you may have noticed in unit 5, optimisation techniques are regarded as the most important techniques in the managerial decision-making processes. An optimisation technique is generally defined as the technique used in finding the value of the independent variable(s) that maximises or minimises the value of the dependent variable.

2.0 Objectives
At the end of this unit, you will be able to:

1. Understand what decision analysis is all about
2. Know how you can make business decisions under conditions of uncertainty
3. Analyse decision problems with a view to providing solutions.
4. Use sample information in making business and economic decisions
5. Be informed about time perspective in business decisions.

3.0 Decision Analysis
Most decision-making situations involve the choice of one among several alternatives actions. The alternative actions and their corresponding payoffs are usually known to the decision-maker in advance. A prospective investor choosing one investment from several alternative investment opportunities, a store owner determining how many of a certain type of commodity to stock, and a company executive making capital-budgeting decisions are some examples of a business decision maker selecting from a multitude of a multitude of alternatives. The decision maker however, does not know which alternative which alternative

will be best in each case, unless he/she also knows with certainty the values of the economic variables that affect profit. These economic variables are referred to, in decision analysis, as *states of nature* as they represent different events that may occur, over which the decision maker has no control.

The states of nature in decision problems are generally denoted by s_i (i = 1, 2, 3, ..., k), where k is the number of or different states of nature in a given business and economic environment. It is assumed here that the states of nature are mutually exclusive, so that no two states can be in effect at the same time, and collectively exhaustive, so that all possible states are included within the decision analysis.

The alternatives available to the decision maker are denoted by a_i (i = 1, 2, 3, ..., n), where n is the number of available alternatives. It is also generally assumed that the alternatives constitute a mutually exclusive, collectively exhaustive set.

3.1 Certainty and Uncertainty in Decision Analysis

When the state if nature, s_i, whether known or unknown, has no influence on the outcomes of given alternatives, we say that the decision maker is operating under *certainty*. Otherwise, he/she is operating under *uncertainty*.

Decision making *under certainty* appears to be simpler than that under uncertainty. Under certainty, the decision maker simply appraises the outcome of each alternative and selects the one that best meets his/her objective. If the number of alternatives is very high however, even in the absence of uncertainty, the best alternative may be difficult to identify. Consider, for example, the problem of a delivery agent who must make 100 deliveries to different residences scattered over Lagos metropolis. There may literally be thousands of different alternative routes the agent could choose. However, if the agent had only 3 stops to make, he/she could easily find the least-cost route.

Decision making *under uncertainty* is always complicated. It is the probability theory and mathematical expectations that offer tools for establishing logical procedures for selecting the best decision alternatives. Though statistics provides the structure for reaching the decision, the decision maker has to inject his/her intuition and knowledge of the problem into the decision-making framework to arrive at the decision that is both theoretically justifiable and intuitively appealing. A good theoretical framework and commonsense approach are both essential ingredients for decision making under uncertainty.
To understand these concepts, consider an investor wishing to invest N100,000 in one of three possible investment alternatives, A, B, and C. Investment A is a Savings Plan with returns of 6 percent annual interest. Investment B is a government bond with 4.5 percent annual interest. Investments A and B involve no risks. Investment C consists of shares of mutual fund with a wide diversity of available holdings from the securities market. The annual return from an

investment in C depends on the uncertain behaviour of the mutual fund under varying economic conditions.

The investors available actions (a_i; I = 1, 2, 3, 4) are as follows
a_1: Do not invest
a_2: Select investment A the 6% bank savings plan.
a_3: Select investment B, the 4.5 % government bond.
a_4: Select investment C, the uncertain mutual fund

Observe that actions a_1 to a_3 do not involve uncertainty as the outcomes associated with them do not depend on uncertain market conditions. Observe also that action a 2 dominates actions a_1 and a_3. In addition, action a_1 is clearly inferior to the risk-free positive growth investment alternatives a_2 and a_3 as it provides for no growth of the principal amount.

Action a_4 is associated with an uncertain outcome that, depending on the state of the economy, may produce either a negative return or a positive return. Thus there exists no apparent dominance relationship between action a_4 and action a_2, the best among the actions involving no uncertainty.

Suppose the investor believes that if the market is down in the next year, an investment in the mutual fund would lose 10 percent returns; if the market stays the same, the investment would stay the same; and if the market is up, the investment would gain 20 percent returns. The investor has thus defined the states of nature for his/her investment decision-making problem as follows:

s_1: The market is down.
s_2: The market remains unchanged.
s_3: The market is up.
A study of the market combined with economic expectations for the coming year may lead the investor to attach subjective probabilities of 0.25, 0.25, and 0.50, respectively, the the states of nature, s_1, s_2, and s_3. The major question is then, how can the investor use the foregoing information regarding investments A, B, and C, and the expected market behaviour serves as an aid in selecting the investment that best satisfies his/her objectives? This question will be considered in the sections that follow.

3.2 Analysis of the Decision Problem
In problems involving choices from many alternatives, one must identify all the actions that may be taken and all the states of nature whose occurrence may influence decisions. The action to take none of the listed alternatives whose outcome is known with certainty may also be included in the list of actions. Associated with each action is a list of payoffs. If an action does not involve risk, the payoff will be the same no matter which state of nature occurs.

The payoffs associated with each possible outcome in a decision problem should be listed in a *payoff table*, defined as a listing, in tabular form, of the value payoffs associated with all possible actions under every state of nature in a decision problem.

The payoff table is usually displayed in grid form, with the states of nature indicated in the columns and the actions in the rows. If the actions are labeled $a_1, a_2, \ldots, a_n$, and the states of nature labeled $s_1, s_2, \ldots, s_k$, a payoff table for a decision problem appears as in table 3.2.1 below. Note that a payoff is entered in each of the nk cells of the payoff table, one for the payoff associated with each action under every possible state of nature.

Table 3.2.1: The Payoff Table

	STATE OF NATURE				
ACTION	s_1	s_2	s_3	...	s_k
a_1					
a_2					
a_3					
. . .					
a_n					

Example

The managing director of a large manufacturing company is considering three potential locations as sites at which to build a subsidiary plant. To decide which location to select for the subsidiary plant, the managing director will determine the degree to which each location satisfies the company's objectives of minimising transportation costs, minimising the effect of local taxation, and having access to an ample pool of available semi-skilled workers. Construct a payoff table and payoff measures that effectively rank each potential location according to the degree to which each satisfies the company's objectives.

Solution
Let the three potential locations be sites A, B, and C. To determine a payoff measure to associate with each of the company's objectives under each alternative, the managing director subjectively assigns a rating on a 0 – to – 10 scale to measure the degree to which each location satisfies the company's objectives. For each objective, a 0 rating indicates complete dissatisfaction, while a 10 rating indicates complete dissatisfaction. The results are presented in table 3.2.2 below:

Table 3.2.2: Ratings for three alternative plant sites for a Manufacturing Company

COMPANY OBJECTIVE	ALTERNATIVE		
	Site A	Site B	Site C
Transportation Costs	6	4	10
Taxation Costs	6	9	5
Workforce Pool	7	6	4

To combine the components of payoff, the managing director asks himself, what are the relative measures of importance of the three company objectives I have considered as components of payoff? Suppose the managing director decides that minimising transportation costs is most important and twice as important as either the minimization of local taxation or the size of workforce available.
He/she thus assigns a weight of 2 to the transportation costs and weights of 1 each to taxation costs and workforce. This will give rise to the following payoff measures:

Payoff (Site A) = 6(2) + 6(1) + 7(1) = 25

Payoff (Site B) = 4(2) + 9(1) + 6(1) = 23

Payoff (Site C) = 10(2) + 5(1) + 4(1) = 29

3.3 Self-Assessment Exercise
Enumerate the major areas of business decision-making. How does the study of managerial economics help a business manager in decision-making?

4.0 Conclusion
This unit focuses on business decision analysis. The idea is that the most plausible way of making business decisions is to look at and analyse business opportunities, variables, and challenges. To help you carry out these important tasks, the unit presents important discussions on:
1. Certainty and uncertainty in decision analysis
2. Analysis of decision problems

5.0 Summary
This unit informs you that most decision-making situations involve the choice of one among several alternatives actions. The alternative actions and their corresponding payoffs are usually known to the decision-maker in advance.
When the state if nature, s_i, whether known or unknown, has no influence on the outcomes of given alternatives, you will say that the decision maker is operating under *certainty*. Otherwise, he/she is operating under *uncertainty*. Decision making *under certainty* appears to be simpler than that under uncertainty. Under certainty, the decision maker simply appraises the outcome of each alternative and selects the one that best meets his/her objective.

In problems involving choices from many alternatives, one must identify all the actions that may be taken and all the states of nature whose occurrence may influence decisions. The action to take none of the listed alternatives whose outcome is known with certainty may also be included in the list of actions. Associated with each action is a list of payoffs. If an action does not involve risk, the payoff will be the same no matter which state of nature occurs.

6.0 Tutor-Marked Assignment

For each of the following business decision-making problems, list the actions available to the decision maker and the states of nature that might result to affect the payoff:

(a) The replacement of manually operated packaging machines by a fully automated machine;

(b) The leasing of a computer by a commercial bank o process checks and handle internal accounting;

(c) The expansion of the market of a brewery from a two-state market to either a four-state market or a seven-state market;

(d) The assignment of seven secretaries to seven executives; and,

(e) The investment of a company pension fund.

7.0 References

Dwivedi, D. N. (2002) *Managerial Economics, sixth edition* (New Delhi: Vikas Publishing House Ltd).

UNIT 7: EXPECTED MONETARY VALUE DECISIONS, DECISION-MAKING INVOLVING SAMPLE INFORMATION, AND TIME PERSPECTIVE IN BUSINESS DECISIONS

Content

1.0 Introduction
2.0 Objectives
3.0 Important Features of Business Decision-Making Processes
3.1 Expected Monetary Value Decisions
3.2 Decision Making Involving Sample Information
3.3 Time Perspective in Business Decisions
3.4 Self-Assessment Exercise
4.0 Conclusion
5.0 Summary
6.0 Tutor-Marked Assignment
7.0 References

1.0 Introduction
As you noted in unit 6, decision analysis provides you with decision-making framework based on available information on the business environment, in the form of either sample information or judgment information or both. In this unit, we examine the important features of business decision making as they relate to expected monetary values, availability of sample information, and time perspective.

2.0 Objectives
Having gone through this unit, you will be able to:

1. Have additional leverage in decision making processes
2. Be informed on how to make expected monetary value decisions
3. Use sample information in profitable business decisions
4. Understand and take into consideration time perspectives in business planning.

3.0 Important Features of Business Decision-Making Processes

3.1 Expected Monetary Value Decisions
A decision-making procedure, which employs both the payoff table and prior probabilities associated with the states of nature to arrive at a decision is referred to as the *Expected Monetary Value* decision procedure. Note that by *prior probability* we mean probabilities representing the chances of occurrence of the identifiable states of nature in a decision problem prior to gathering any sample information. The *expected monetary value decision* refers to the selection of available action based on either the expected opportunity loss or the expected profit of the action.

Decision makers are generally interested in the *optimal monetary value decisions*. The optimal expected monetary value decision involves the selection of the action associated with the minimum *expected opportunity loss* or the action associated with the maximum *expected profit*, depending on the objective of the decision maker.

The concept of expected monetary value applies mathematical expectation, where opportunity loss or profit is the random variable and the prior probabilities represent the probability distribution associated with the random variable.

The **expected opportunity loss** is computed by:

$$E(L_i) = \sum_{all\ j} L_{ij} P(s_j), \qquad (i = 1, 2, ..., n)$$

where L_{ij} is the opportunity loss for selecting action a_i given that the state of nature, s_j, occurs and $P(s_j)$ is the prior probability assigned to the state of nature, s_j.

The **expected profits** for each action is computed in a similar way:

$$E(\pi_i) = \sum_{all\ j} \pi_{ij} P(s_j)$$

where π_{ij} represents profits for selecting action a_i

Example

By recording the daily demand for a perishable commodity over a period of time, a retailer was able to construct the following probability distribution for the daily demand levels:

Table 3.1.1: Probability Distribution for the Daily Demand

s_j	$P(s_j)$
1	0.5
2	0.3
3	0.2
4 or more	0.0

The opportunity loss table for this demand-inventory situation is as follows:

Table 3.1.2: The Opportunity Loss Table

Action, Inventory	State of Nature, Demand		
	$s_1(1)$	$s_2(2)$	$s_3(3)$
$a_1(1)$	0	3	6
$a_2(2)$	2	0	3
$a_3(3)$	4	2	0

We are required to find the inventory level that minimises the expected opportunity loss.

Solution
Given the prior probabilities in the first table, the expected opportunity loss are computed as follows:

$E(L_i) = \sum_{j=1}^{3} L_{ij} P(s_j)$, for each inventory level, $I = 1, 2, 3$.

The expected opportunity losses at each inventory level become:

$E(L_1) = 0(0.5) + 3(0.3) + 6(0.2) = N2.10$

$E(L_2) = 2(0.5) + 0(0.3) + 3(0.2) = N1.60$

$E(L_3) = 4(0.5) + 2(0.3) + 0(0.2) = N2.60$

It follows that in order to minimize the expected opportunity loss, the retailer should stock 2 units of the perishable commodity. This is the optimal decision.

3.2 Decision Making Involving Sample Information

In discussing prior probabilities, recall it was noted that prior probabilities are acquired either by subjective selection or by computation from historical data. No current information describing the probability of occurrence of the states of nature was assumed to be available.

In many cases, observational information or other evidence are available to the decision maker either for purchase or at the cost of experimentation. For example, a retailer whose business depends on the weather may consult a meteorologist before making decisions, or an investor may hire a market consultant before investing. Market surveys carried out before the release of a new product represent another area in which the decision maker may seek additional information. In each of these examples, the decision maker attempts to acquire information relative to the occurrence of the states of nature from a source other than that from which the prior probabilities were computed.

When such information are available, *Baye's Law* can be employed to revise the prior probabilities to reflect the new information. These revised probabilities are referred to as *posterior probabilities*.

By definition, the *posterior probability* represented symbolically by $P(s_k/x)$ is the probability of occurrence of the state of nature s_k, given the sample information, x. This probability is computed by:

$$P(s_k/x) = \frac{P(x/s_k)P(s_k)}{\sum_{\text{all } i} P(x/s_i)P(s_i)}$$

The probabilities, $P(x/s_i)$ are the conditional probabilities of observing the observational information, x, under the states of nature, s_i, and the probabilities $P(s_i)$ are the prior probabilities.

The expected monetary value decisions are formulated in the same way as before, except that the posterior probabilities are used instead of prior probabilities. If the objective is to minimize the expected opportunity loss, the quantity is computed for each action ai. The expected opportunity loss in this case is computed by:

$$E(L_i) = \sum_{all\ I} L_{ij} P(s_i/x) \quad I = 1, 2, 3, \ldots, n$$

Example
It is known that an assembly machine operates at a 5 percent or 10 percent defective rate. When running at a 10 percent defective rate, the machine is said to be out of control. It is then shut down and readjusted. From past experience, the machine is known to run at 5 percent defective rate 90 percent of the time. A sample of size n = 20 has been selected from the output of the machine, and y = 2 defectives have been observed. Based on both the prior and sample information, what is the probability that the assembly machine is in control (running at 5 percent defective rate)?

Solution
The states of nature in this example relates to the assembly machine defective rates. Thus the states of nature include:
$s_1 = 0.05$, and $s_2 = 0.10$ with the assumed prior probabilities of occurrence of 0.90 and 0.10. We are required to use these prior probabilities, in line with the observed sample information, to find the posterior probability associated with the state of nature, s_1.

In this problem, the "experimental information, x" is the observation of y = 2 defectives from a sample of n = 20 items selected from the output of the assembly machine. We need to find the probability that the experimental information, x, could arise under each state of nature, s_i. This can be done by referring to the binomial probability distribution table found in the appendix.

Under the state of nature $s_1 = 0.05$, we obtain:

P(x/0.05) = P(n = 20, y =2/0.05) = 0.925 – 0.736 = 0.189 (from the binomial distribution table)
Under the state of nature, $s_2 = 0.10$, we obtain:

P(x/0.10) = P(n = 20, y = 2/0.10) = 0.677 – 0.392 = 0.285 (from the binomial distribution table).

We now employ the Baye's Law to find the posterior probability that the machine is in control (s_1) based on both the prior and experimental information. To make the work easy, we use the Columnar approach to the use of Baye's Law as illustrated below:

Table 3.2.1: Columnar Approach to Use of Baye's Law

	(1) State of Nature, s_i	(2) Prior, $P(s_i)$	(3) Experimental Information, $P(x/s_i)$	(4) Product, $P(s_i)P(x/s_i)$	(5) Posterior, $P(s_i/x)$
s_1	0.05	0.90	0.189	0.1701	0.86
s_2	0.10	0.10	0.285	0.0285	0.14
		1.00		0.1986	1.00

Looking at column (4), we observe the product of the entries in columns (2) and (3). These values measure the *joint probabilities*. The sum of the entries in column (4) is the term in the denominator of the formula for Baye's Law and measures the *marginal probability* of observing the experimental information, x. The posterior probabilities, column (5), are obtained by taking each entry in column (4) and dividing by the sum of the entries in column (4).

Even though we found that 10 percent of the items in the sample is defective (that is, 2 out of the 20 items is defective), the posterior probability that the machine is running at the 10 percent defective rate (running out of control) is only 0.14, which is a little greater than the prior probability that the machine is out of control (0.10). It follows that the probability that the machine is not running out of control is 0.86.

3.3 Time Perspective in Business Decisions

All business decisions are taken with some time perspective. Time perspective refers to the duration of time period extending from the relevant past to foreseeable future, taken into consideration while making a business decision. The relevant past refers to the period of past experience and trends which are relevant for business decisions with long-run implications. Bear in mind that all business decisions do not have the same time perspective. Some have short-run repercussions, and therefore, involve short-run perspective. For instance, a decision regarding building inventories of finished product involves a short-run time perspective.

There are many business decisions which have long-run repercussions such as, investment in land, building, machinery, expansion of the scale of production, introduction of a new product, investment abroad, and the like. Decisions on such business issues may not be profitable in the short-run, but may prove very profitable in the long-run.

Business decisions makers must therefore, assess and determine the time perspective of business propositions well in advance and make decisions accordingly. Determination of time perspective is very significant, especially where forecasting, planning, and projections are involved. Decision-makers must decide on an appropriate future period for projecting the value of a given business variable. Otherwise, projections may prove meaningless from business analysis point of view and decisions based thereon may result in poor pay-offs. For instance, in a business decision regarding the establishment of an institute of entrepreneurship, projecting a short-run demand and taking a short-run time perspective will not be wise.

3.4 Self-Assessment Exercise
Give the justification for using an expected monetary value objective in decision problems.

4.0 Conclusion
To beef up your understanding of business decision-making processes, this unit has examined the important features of decision making in business, including:
1. Expected monetary value decisions
2. Decisions involving sample information
3. Time perspective in business decisions

5.0 Summary
Decision makers are generally interested in the *optimal monetary value decisions*. The optimal expected monetary value decision involves the selection of the action associated with the minimum *expected opportunity loss* or the action associated with the maximum *expected profit*, depending on the objective of the decision maker.

All business decisions are taken with some time perspective. Time perspective refers to the duration of time period extending from the relevant past to foreseeable future, taken into consideration while making a business decision. The relevant past refers to the period of past experience and trends which are relevant for business decisions with long-run implications.

6.0 Tutor-Marked Assignment
A business person is trying to decide whether to take one of two contracts or neither one. He/she has simplified the situation and feels it is sufficient to imagine that the contracts provide the alternatives shown in the following table:

ContractA		ContractB	
Profit	Probability	Profit	Probability
N100,000	0.20		
50,000	0.40	N40,000	0.30
0	0.30	10,000	0.40
-30,000	0.10	-10,000	0.30

(a) Which contract should the business person select if he/she wishes to maximize his/her expected profit?
(b) What is the expected profit associated with the optimal decision?

7.0 References

Dwivedi, D. N. (2002) *Managerial Economics, sixth edition* (New Delhi: Vikas Publishing House Ltd).

UNIT 8: ANALYSIS OF MARKET DEMAND

Content
1.0 Introduction
2.0 Objectives
3.0 Analysis of Market Demand
3.1 Definition of Market Demand

3.2 Types of Demand
3.3 Determinants of Market Demand
3.4 Self-Assessment Exercise
4.0 Conclusion
5.0 Summary
6.0 Tutor-Marked Assignment
7.0 References

1.0 Introduction

This unit discusses the meaning of market demand, types of demand, determinants of market demand, the demand functions, elasticities of demand, and techniques of demand forecasting. This is in recognition of the fact that the analysis of market demand for a business firm's product plays an important role in business decision making. In addition, for a firm to succeed in its operations, it must plan for future production, the inventories of raw materials, advertisements, and sales outlets. It follows that the knowledge of the magnitude of the current and future demand is indispensable.

The analysis of market demand enables business executives know:
  6. the factors determining the size of consumer demand for their products;
  7. the degree of responsiveness of demand to changes in its determinants;
  8. the possibility of sales promotion through manipulation of prices;
  9. responsiveness of demand to advertisement expenditures; and,
  10. optimum levels of sales, inventories, and advertisement expenditures.

2.0 Objectives

At the end of this unit, you should be able to:
1. Know what the market demand is all about
2. Understand the various types of demand
3. Be familiar with the determinants of demand

3.0 Analysis of Market Demand

3.1 Definition of Market Demand
The market demand of any product is the sum of individual demands for the product at a given market price in a given time period. Note that the individual demand for the product per unit of time at a given price is the quantity demanded by an individual.

A horizontal summation of individual demand schedule gives rise to the *market demand schedule.* For example, assume three consumers, X, Y, and Z of a given commodity, say commodity A. Let the individual demands by the consumers, X, Y, and Z be represented as in table 3.1 below, the market demand schedule, that is, the aggregate of individual demands by the three consumers at different prices, as indicated, is shown by the last column of the table.

Table 3.1.1: The Market Demand Schedule

Price of A	Quantity of A Demanded by:			Market Demand
	X	Y	Z	
10	5	1	0	6
8	7	2	0	9
6	10	4	1	15
4	14	6	2	22
2	20	10	4	34
0	27	15	8	50

3.2 Types of Demand
The major types of demand encountered in business decisions are outlined below.

3.2.1. Individual and Market Demand.
The quantity of a commodity an individual is willing and able to purchase at a particular price, during a specific time period, given his/her money income, his/her taste, and prices of other commodities, such as substitutes and complements, is referred to as the *individual demand* for the commodity. As illustrated in table 3.1 above, the total quantity which all the consumers of the commodity are willing and able to purchase at a given price per time unit, given their money incomes, their tastes, and prices of other commodities, is referred to as the *market demand* for the commodity.

3.2.2. Demand for firm's and Industry's Product.
The quantity of a firm's product that can be sold at a given price over time is known as the demand for the firm's product. The sum of demand for the products of all firms in the industry is referred to as the market demand or industry demand for the product.

3.2.3 Autonomous and Derived Demand.
An *autonomous demand* or direct demand for a commodity is one that arises on its own out of a natural desire to consume or possess a commodity. This type of demand is independent of the demand for other commodities. Autonomous demand may also arise due to *demonstration effect* of a rise in income, increase in population, and advertisement of new products.

The demand for a commodity which arises from the demand for other commodities, called *'parent products'* is called *derived demand*. Demand for land, fertilizers and agricultural tools, is a derived demand because these commodities are demanded due to demand for food. In addition, demand for bricks, cement, and the like are derived demand from the demand for house and other types of buildings. In general, demand for producer goods or industrial inputs is a derived demand.

3.2.4 Demand for Durable and Non-Durable Goods.
Durable goods are those goods for which the total utility or usefulness is not exhaustible in the short-run use. Such goods can be used repeatedly over a period of time. Durable consumer goods include houses, clothing, shoes, furniture, refrigerator, and the like.

Durable producer goods include mainly the items under 'fixed assets', such as building, plant, machinery, and office furniture.

The demand for durable goods changes over a relatively longer period than that of the non-durable goods. The demand for non-durable goods depends largely on their current prices, consumers' income, and fashion. It is also subject to frequent changes.

Durable goods create replacement demand, while non-durable goods do not. In addition, the demand for non-durable goods change linearly, while the demand the demand for durable goods change exponentially as the stock of durable goods changes.

3.2.5. Short-term and Long-term Demand.
Short-term demand refers to the demand for goods over a short period. The type of goods involved in the short-term demand are most fashion **consumer goods, goods used seasonally, inferior substitutes for superior goods during scarcities.** Short-**term demand depends mainly on the commodity price, price of their substitutes, current disposable** income of the consumers, the consumers' ability to adjust their consumption pattern, and their susceptibility to advertisement of new products.

The *long-term demand* refers to the demand which exists over a long period of time. Changes in long-term demand occur only after a long period. Most generic goods have long-term demand. The long-term demand depends on the long-term income trends, availability of better substitutes, sales promotion, consumer credit facility, and the like.

3.3 Determinants of Market Demand

For corporate managers at large and specifically, the marketing managers, it is highly important to understand the factors affecting the market demand for their products. This understanding is required for analysing and estimating demand for the products. Though there are several factors affecting market demand for a product, the most important are:
1. *Price of the product or the own price (Po).* This is the most important determinant of demand for a product. The own price of a product and the quantity demanded of it are inversely-related so that,

$$\frac{\Delta Qo}{\Delta Po} > 0$$

2. *Price of the related goods, such as substitutes and complements (Ps and Pc)* When two goods are *substitutes* for each other, the change in price of one affects the demand for the other in the same direction. If goods X and Y are substitute goods, then an increase in the price of X will give rise to an increase in the demand for Y. Note that changes in the price of related goods cause shifts in the demand for the goods. Changes in demand are illustrated graphically as rightward shifts (for increase) and leftward shifts (for decrease) in the demand for the products. As shown below, An increase in the price of good X will shift the demand for good Y to the right and shift that of good X to the left.

Figure 3.3.1: Shifts in Demand

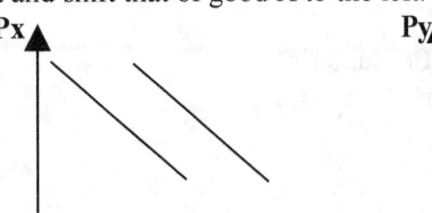

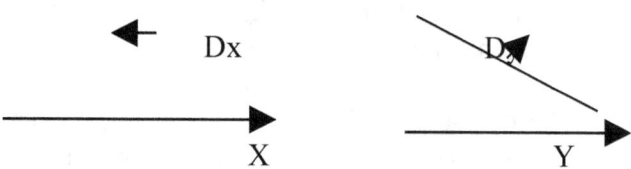

Symbolically, $D_x = f(P_y)$; $\Delta D_x/\Delta P_y > 0$

$D_y = f(P_x)$; $\Delta D_y/\Delta P_x > 0$

When two goods are complements for each other, one complements the use of another. Petrol and car a complement goods. If an increase in the price of one good causes a decrease in demand for the other, the goods are said to be complements. Thus if the demand function for a car (Dc) in relation to petrol price (Pp) is specified by:

$D_c f(P_p)$, $\Delta D_c/\Delta P_p < 0$.

3. **Consumer's Income** This is the major determinant of demand for any product since the purchasing power of the consumer is determined by the disposable income. Managers need to know that income-demand relationship is of a more varied nature than those between demand and its other determinants.

The relationship between demand for commodity X, for example, and the consumer's income, say Y, keeping other factors constant, can be expressed by a demand function:
$D_x = f(Y)$, and $\Delta D_x/\Delta Y > 0$.

You should note that consumer goods of different nature have different relationships with income of different categories of consumers. The manager needs, therefore, to be completely aware of the goods they deal with and their relationship with consumer's income, particularly with respect to the assessment of both existing and prospective demand for a product.

Regarding income-demand analysis, consumer goods and services are grouped under *four* broad categories:

i. **Essential Consumer Goods (ECG).** Goods and services in this category are referred to as 'basic needs', and are consumed by all persons in a society. Such goods and services include food grains, salt, vegetable oil, cooking, fuel, housing, and minimum clothing. The demand for such goods and services increase with increases in consumer's income, but only up to a certain limit, even though the total expenditure may increase in accordance with the quality of goods consumed, all things being equal. The relationship between goods and services of this category and consumer's income is shown by the curve ECG in figure 3.3.2 below.

Figure 3.3.2: Income-Demand Relationships

Consumer's

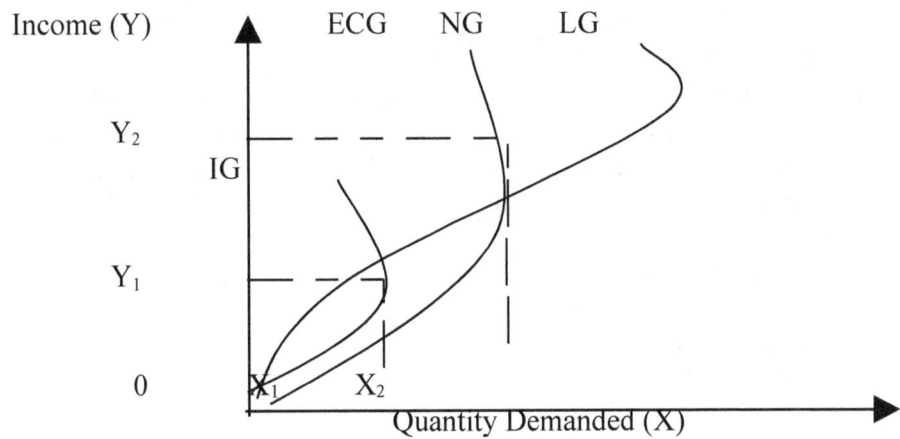

ii. *Inferior Goods (IG).* Inferior and superior goods are widely known to both buyers and sellers. Economists define inferior goods as goods in which their demands decrease as consumer's income increases, beyond a certain level of income. The relationship between income and demand for an inferior good is illustrated by curve IG in figure 3.3.2 above. Demand for such goods rises only up to a certain level of income, say (OY_1), and declines as income increases beyond this level.

iii. *Normal Goods (NG).* In economic terms, normal goods are goods demanded in increasing quantities as consumer's income rises. Examples of normal goods are clothing, furniture, and automobiles. The type of relationship between income and demand for normal goods is shown by curve NG in figure 3.3.2 above. Note in the figure that up to a certain level of income, say Y_1, the relationship between income and demand for all types of goods is similar. The difference is only in terms of the degree of relationship. The relationship becomes distinctively different beyond the income level (Y_1).

iv. *Luxury and Prestige Goods.* All such goods that add to the pleasure and prestige of the consumer without enhancing his or her earning fall in the category of luxury goods. Prestige goods are special category of luxury goods, examples, rare paintings and antiques, prestigious schools, and the like. Demand for such goods arises beyond a certain level of consumer's income. Producers of such goods, while assessing the demand for their product, need to consider the income changes in the richer section of the society. The income-demand relationship for this category of goods is shown by curve LG in figure 3.3.2.

4. Consumers' Tastes and Preferences Consumers' tastes and preferences play important role in the determination of the demand for a product. Tastes and preferences generally depend on life style, social customs, religious values attached to a commodity, habit of the people, age and sex of the consumers, and the like. Changes in these factors tend to change consumers' tastes and preferences.

5. Advertisement Expenditures. Advertisement costs are incurred while attempting to promote sales. It helps in increasing product demands in at least four ways:
(a) by informing the potential consumers about the product's availability;

(b) by showing the product's superiority over the rival product;
(c) by influencing consumer's choice against the rival product; and,
(d) by setting new fashions and changing tastes. The impact of these causes upward shifts in the demand for the product. All things being equal, as expenditure on advertisement increases, it is expected that volume of sales will increase. The relationship between sales (S) and advertisement outlays (AD) can be expressed by the function:
S = f(AD), and ∆S/∆AD > 0. This relationship is indicated in figure 3.3.3 below:

Figure 3.3.3 Advertisement and Sales

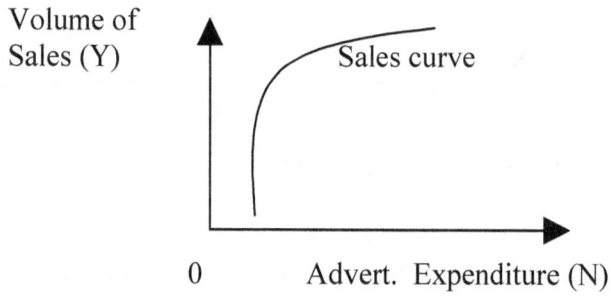

The relationship as shown by figure 3.3.3 is based on the following assumptions:
  (a) Consumers are fairly sensitive and responsive to various modes of advertisement
  (b) The rival firms do not react to the advertisement made by the firm,
  (c) The level of demand has not reached the saturation point and advertisement makes only marginal impact on demand for a product,
  (d) Adding of advertisement cost to the product price does not make the price prohibitive for consumers, compared to the price of substitutes.

6. Consumers' Expectations. The consumers' expectations about the future product prices, income, and supply position of goods play significant role in the determination of demand for goods and services in the short run. A rational consumer who expects a high rise in the price of a nonperishable commodity would buy more of it at the high current price with a view to avoiding the pinch of the high price rise in the future. This partly explains the high demand for fuel during periods of expected increase of pump price of fuel in Nigeria. On the contrary, if a rational consumer expects a fall in the price of goods he/she purchases, he/she would postpone the purchase of such goods with a view to taking advantage of lower prices in the future. This is especially the case for non-essential goods. This behaviour tends to reduce the current demand for goods whose prices are expected to decrease in the future.

An expected increase in income would similarly increase current demand for goods and services. For instance, a corporate announcement of bonuses or upward revision of salary scales would induce increases in current demand for goods and services.

7. Demonstration Effect. Whenever new commodities or models of commodities are introduced in the market, many households buy them not because of their genuine need for them but because their neighbours have purchased them. This type of purchase arises out of such feelings jealousy, competition, and equality in the peer group, social inferiority, and the desire to raise once social status. Purchases based on these factors are the result of what economists refer to as 'demonstration effect' or the 'Band-Wagon effect'. These effects have positive impacts on commodity demand.

On the contrary, when a commodity becomes a thing of common use, some rich people decrease their consumption of such goods. This behaviour is referred to in economics as the 'snob effect'. This has negative impact on the demand for the commodity concerned.

Other determinants of demand for commodities include *Consumer-Credit facility*, the *population of consumers*, and *income distribution*.

3.4 Self-Assessment Exercise
Briefly discuss the reason it is important for a manager to understand the various types of demand.

4.0 Conclusion
This unit has defined a product's market demand as the sum of individual demands for the product. In addition, you were informed that a horizontal sum of individual demand schedule will result in the market demand schedule.

The unit presents five different types of demand: (i) individual and market demand; (ii) demand for firm's and industry product; (iii) autonomous and derived demand; (iv) demand for durable and non-durable goods; and, (v) short-term and long-term demand.

You also learned that the determinants of demand include: the product's own price; price of related goods; consumer tastes; consumer income; consumer expectations; and others.

5.0 Summary
The market demand of any product is the sum of individual demands for the product at a given market price in a given time period. The individual demand for the product per unit of time at a given price is the quantity demanded by an individual.

The quantity of a commodity an individual is willing and able to purchase at a particular price, during a specific time period, given his/her money income, his/her taste, and prices of other commodities, such as substitutes and complements, is referred to as the ***individual demand*** for the commodity.

An *autonomous demand* or direct demand for a commodity is one that arises on its own, out of a natural desire to consume or possess a commodity. This type of demand is independent of the demand for other commodities. Autonomous demand may also arise due to *demonstration effect* of a rise in income, increase in population, and advertisement of new products.

Durable goods are those goods for which the total utility or usefulness is not exhaustible in the short-run use. Such goods can be used repeatedly over a period of time. The demand for durable goods changes over a relatively longer period than that of the non-durable goods.

Consumer goods of different nature have different relationships with income of different categories of consumers. The manager needs, therefore, to be completely aware of the goods they deal with and their relationship with consumer's income, particularly with respect to the assessment of both existing and prospective demand for a product.

6.0 Tutor-Marked Assignment
Explain with practical examples the following demand concepts:
1. Autonomous demand
2. Industry demand
3. Demonstration or Band-Wagon effect on demand

7.0 References
Dwivedi, D. N. (2002) ***Managerial Economics, sixth edition*** (New Delhi: Vikas Publishing House Ltd).

UNIT 9: DEMAND FUNCTIONS

Content
1.0 Introduction
2.0 Objectives
3.0 The Demand functions
3.1 Linear Demand function
3.2 Nonlinear Demand Function

3.3 Multi-Variate or Dynamic Demand Function
3.4 Self-Assessment Exercise
4.0 Conclusion
5.0 Summary
6.0 Tutor-Marked Assignment
7.0 References

1.0 Introduction
Mathematically, we can define a function as a symbolic representation of relationship between dependent and independent variables. A demand function states the relationship between the demand for a product (the dependent variable in this case) and its determinants (the independent variables).

It is the nature of demand-price relationship that determines the form of a demand function. The three most common forms of demand functions are the *linear demand function*, *non-linear demand function* and the *multi-variate or dynamic demand function*. Each of these forms will be presented briefly in the following discussions.

2.0 Objectives
Having gone through the discussions in this unit, you should be able to:
1. Be informed about the theoretical demand functions
2. Understand the differences between the various types of demand functions
3. Know the principles behind modeling of demand for goods and services

3.0 The Demand functions
The various types of demand functions relevant to our discussions include:
1. The Linear Demand function;
2. The non-linear demand function; and,
3. The multivariate or dynamic demand function.

Each of these demand functions has specific roles to play in decision making involving the demand for a firm's product.

3.1 Linear Demand function
A demand function is said to be linear when its graph results in a straight line. The general form of a linear demand function is presented in equation (3.1.1) below:
$$D_x = a - bP_x \qquad (3.1.1)$$
Where a = the demand intercept or the quantity demanded at a zero price,

b = the slope of the demand function or the rate at which quantity demanded of product X changes with respect to the price (P_x). This slope is defined by $\Delta D_x/\Delta P_x$

The graphical form of this demand function is illustrated in figure 3.1.1 below.

Figure 3.1.1: Linear Demand Function

Price
(P_x)

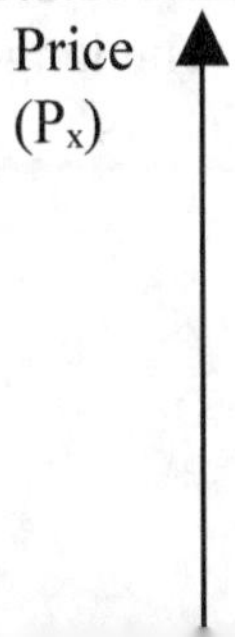

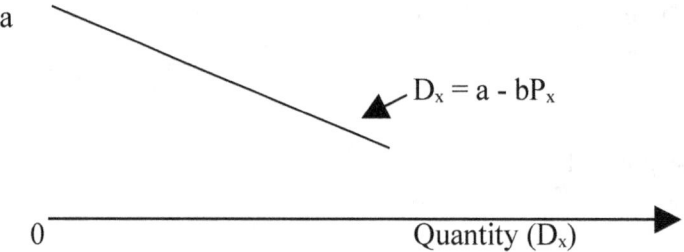

The price function can easily be obtained from the demand function (equation 3.1.1) in the following way:

$D_x = a - bP_x$

$bP_x = a - D_x$

$$P_x = \frac{a - D_x}{b} = \frac{a}{b} - \frac{1}{b}D_x \qquad (3.1.2)$$

3.2 Nonlinear Demand Function

A demand function is said to be nonlinear or curvilinear when the slope of the of the demand function, $\Delta P/\Delta D$, changes along the demand curve. A nonlinear demand function yields a demand curve unlike the demand line yielded by a linear demand function as in figure 3.1.1 above. A nonlinear demand function is of the form of a power function as given in equation (3.2.1) below.

$$D_x = aP_x^{-b} \qquad (3.2.1)$$

You should note that the exponent of the Price variable P_x, that is, $-b$, in the nonlinear demand function (equation (3.2.1) is referred to as the price-elasticity of demand. The nonlinear demand function can be sketched as in figure 3.2.1 below.

Figure 3.2.1: Nonlinear Demand Function

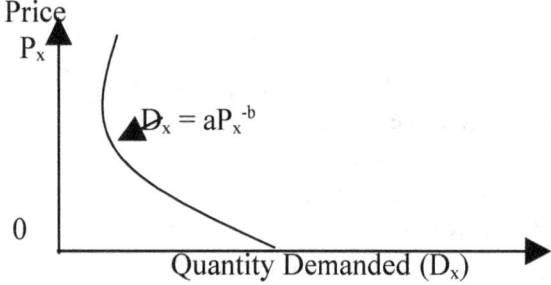

3.3 Multi-Variate or Dynamic Demand Function

The demand functions discussed above are classified as single-variable demand functions, and, as such, referred to as short-term demand functions. In the long run, neither the individual nor the market demand for a given product is determined by anyone of its determinants alone, because other determinants do not remain constant. The long-run demand for a product depends on the composite impact of all its determinants operating simultaneously. It follows that in order to estimate the long-term demand for a product, all the relevant determinants must be taken into account.

The long-run demand functions describe the relationship between a demand for a product (the dependent variable) and its determinants (the independent variables). Demand functions of this type are referred to as *multi-variate* or *dynamic* demand functions. Consider the demand for product X, (D_x), which depends on such variables as its own price (P_x), consumer's income (Y), price of its substitutes (P_s), price of the complementary goods (P_c), consumer's taste (T), and advertisement expenditure (A), the functional form can be written as:

$$D_x = f(P_x, Y, P_s, P_c, T, A) \qquad (3.3.1)$$

If the relationship between the demand (D_x) and the quantifiable independent variables, P_x, Y, P_s, P_c, and A, is of a linear form, then the estimable form of the demand function is formulated as:

$$D_x = a + bP_x + cY + dP_s + eP_c + gA \qquad (3.3.2)$$

where 'a' is a constant and parameters b, c, d, e. and g are the coefficients of relationship between the demand for product X (D_x) and the respective independent variables.

For the market demand function for a product, other independent variables such as size of the population (N), and a measure of income distribution, the Gini-coefficient (G) may be included in equation (3.3.2).

3.4 Self-Assessment Exercise Briefly present the major determinant of the form of a firm's demand function.

4.0 Conclusion
You can define a demand function as a symbolic representation of relationship between the demand for a product and its determinants. When established, this relationship can help you predict what will happen to the demand for your product when the determinants of the demand changes. A demand function can take any of the following forms: (i) linear; non-linear; or multivariate.

5.0 Summary
You have learned from this unit that:
1. It is extremely important for a manager to understand the relationship between product's demand and its determinants.
2. It is the nature of demand-price relationship that determines the form of the demand function for a product.
3. The major forms of demand function include:

(i) The linear demand function represented by the equation:
$$D_x = a - bP_x$$
(ii) A nonlinear demand function which is of the form of a power function given as:

$$D_x = aP_x^{-b}$$

(iii) The multivariate or dynamic demand function, which takes into account all the relevant determinants of demand.

6.0 Tutor-Marked Assignment

You are required to discuss, with relevant examples, the various forms of a demand function.

References

Dwivedi, D. N. (2002) *Managerial Economics, sixth edition* (New Delhi: Vikas Publishing House Ltd).

UNIT 10: ELASTICITY OF DEMAND

Content
1.0 Introduction
2.0 Objectives
3.0 Elasticity of Demand
3.1 Own –Price Elasticity of Demand

3.2 Cross-Elasticity of Demand
3.3 Determinants of Price-elasticity of demand
3.4 Measuring Price-Elasticity of Demand from a Demand Function
3.5 Self-Assessment Exercise
4.0 Conclusion
5.0 Summary
6.0 Tutor-Marked Assignment
7.0 References

1.0 Introduction
From the managerial point of view, the knowledge of the nature of relationship between product's demand and its determinants is not sufficient. What is more important is the degree of responsiveness of demand to changes in its determinants. This degree of responsiveness of demand to changes in its determinants is referred to as *the elasticity of demand* for the product in question.

The concept of elasticity of demand plays significant role in pricing decisions. In practical business decisions, firms would like to pass cost increases over to the consumers through price increases. But whether increase in price as a result of rising cost is beneficial to the firm will depend on:
5. the price-elasticity of demand for the product; and,
6. the price-elasticity of demand for its substitutes

Raising the price may be beneficial if:
(i) demand for a product is less elastic; and,
(ii) demand for its substitute is much less elastic.

This unit discusses the various methods of measuring price elasticity of demand. The concepts of price-elasticities of demand mostly used in business decisions are:
(i) Own- Price Elasticity,
(ii) Cross-Price Elasticity,

2.0 Objectives
At the end of this unit, you must have:
1. Been able to define the elasticity of demand
2. Learned the different types of demand elasticities used in business decisions
3. Learned how to apply the concepts of demand elasticities in making production and distribution decisions.

3.0 Elasticity of Demand
The elasticity of demand concepts are presented as follows:

3.1 Own –Price Elasticity of Demand
The own-price elasticity of demand is generally defined as the degree of responsiveness of demand for a commodity to changes in its own price. More precisely, it is the

percentage change in quantity demanded as a result of *one* percent change in the price of the commodity. The working definition is as follows:

$$e_p = \frac{\text{Percentage change in quantity demanded (Q)}}{\text{Percentage change in price (P)}}$$

where e_p stands for own-price elasticity.

From this definition, a general formula for the calculation of the coefficient of own-price elasticity is derived as follows:

$$e_p = \frac{\Delta Q}{Q} \div \frac{\Delta P}{P} = \frac{\Delta Q}{Q} \times \frac{P}{\Delta P}$$

$$= \frac{\Delta Q}{\Delta P} \times \frac{P}{Q} \qquad (3.1.1)$$

where Q = original quantity demand, P = original price, ΔQ = change in quantity demanded (new quantity – original quantity), ΔP = change in price (new price – original price).

Note that since the term, $\Delta Q/\Delta P$, is the slope of the demand function, a minus sign (-) is generally inserted in the formula (3.1.1) before the fraction with a view to making the elasticity coefficient a non-negative value.

The own-price elasticity can be measured between two points on a demand curve (for *arc elasticity*) or on a point (for *point elasticity*).

3.1.1 Arc Elasticity
An arc elasticity measures the elasticity of demand between any two finite points on a given demand line or curve. Measure of elasticity between points A and B in figure 3.6 below, for example, is referred to as arc elasticity. Movement from point A to B indicates a fall in the commodity price from say, N10/unit to N8/unit, so that $\Delta P = N(10 - 8) = N2$. The decrease in price is assumed to cause an increase in quantity demanded from say, 50 to 60 units, so that $\Delta Q = 50 - 60 = -10$ units. The elasticity from A to B can be computed by substituting these values into the elasticity formula to get:

$e_p = -\Delta Q/\Delta P \cdot P_o/Q_o$ (P_o = original price; Q_o = original quantity)

$= -10/2 \times 10/50 = -1$ (the case of unitary elasticity)

The elasticity of 1 (unitary elasticity) implies that 1 percent decrease in price of the commodity results in 1 percent increase in quantity demanded.

Figure 3.1.1: Arc Elasticity for a Linear Demand Function

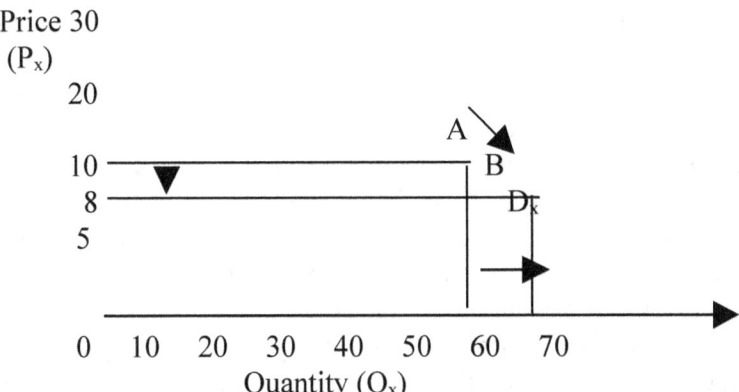

It is important to note that one problem associated with the use of arc elasticity is that the elasticity coefficient changes along the demand line or curve as the direction of price change is reversed, say from price decrease to price increase in our present example. To confirm this, try re-computing the arc elasticity if price rises from N8/unit to N10/unit, instead.

3.1.2 Point Elasticity

Point elasticity is the elasticity of demand at a finite point on a demand line or a demand curve. For example, at the point C or D on the linear demand line, MN, of figure 3.1.2, you will calculate the point elasticity. This is not the same as the arc elasticity between points C and D.

Figure 3.1.2: Point Elasticity for a Linear Demand Function

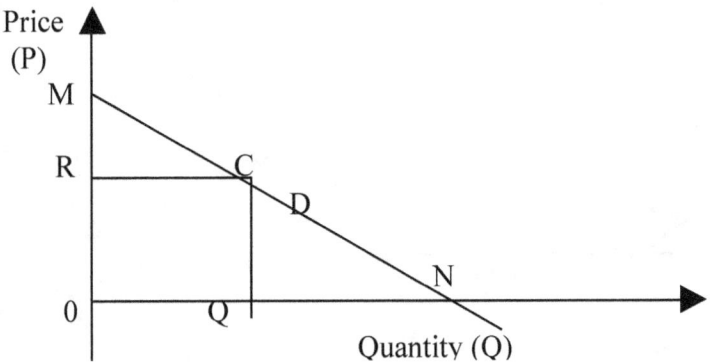

A movement from point D towards C would imply change in Price (ΔP) becoming smaller and smaller, such that point C is almost approached. At this point, the change in price is infinitesimally small. The measurement of elasticity for an infinitesimally small change in price is same as measurement of elasticity at a point. Point elasticity is measured by the following formula:

Point elasticity (e_p) = (P/Q)(dQ/dP)

The derivative, dQ/dP, is reciprocal of the slope of the demand line or demand curve, that is, 1/dP/dQ.

3.1.3 Point elasticity on a Non-Linear Demand Curve.

It is worthy of note that the ratio $\Delta D/\Delta P$ in respect of a non-linear demand curve (function) is different at each point on the curve. It follows that the technique used in measuring point elasticity on a linear demand function (line) can not be directly applied. To measure point elasticity on a non-linear demand curve, the chosen point is first transformed or imposed on a linear demand line. This can be done by drawing a tangent line through the chosen point on the non-linear curve. In figure 3.1.3, suppose for example, you want to measure elasticity on the non-linear demand curve, DD, at point C, you need to draw a line MN tangent to the curve through the point, C. Since the line MN passes through the same point, C as the non-linear demand curve, DD, the slope of the line and the demand curve at point C is the same. Thus, the elasticity of the demand curve at point C will be equal to that of the line at this point. The elasticity of the line at point C can be computed as:

$$e_p = \frac{P}{Q} \cdot \frac{dQ}{dP}$$

$$= \frac{CQ}{0Q} \cdot \frac{QN}{CQ} = \frac{QN}{0Q}$$

Figure 3.1.3: Measuring Elasticity on Non-Linear Demand Curve

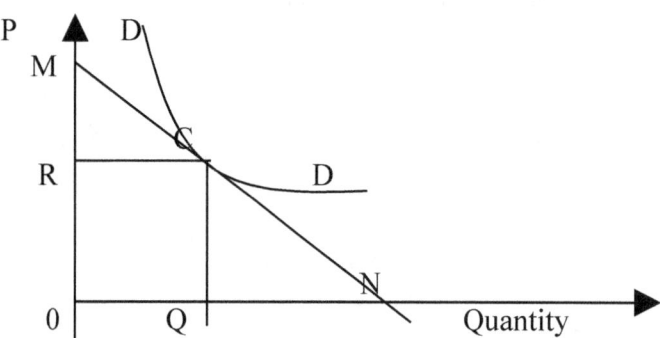

3.2: Cross-Elasticity of Demand

The cross-elasticity (or cross-price elasticity) can be defined as the degree of responsiveness of demand for a commodity to the changes in price of its substitutes and complementary goods. The formula for measuring the cross-elasticity of demand for a commodity, X, can be written as:

$$E_{x,i} = \frac{\text{Percentage change in quantity demanded of X } (Q_x)}{\text{Percentage change in the price of i } (P_i)}$$

$$= \frac{P_i \cdot \Delta Q_x}{} \qquad\qquad (3.2.1)$$

$Q_x \quad \Delta P_i$

where i refers to either substitutes to commodity X or its complementary goods.

The cross-elasticity of demand can be used to identify substitute and complementary goods for a given commodity. If the cross-price elasticity between two goods is positive, the two goods may be considered as substitutes to one another. The greater the cross-price elasticity coefficient, the closer the substitute. Similarly, if the cross-price elasticity is negative, the two goods may be considered as complements. The higher the negative cross-elasticity coefficient, the higher the degree of complementarity.

The concept of cross-elasticity is important in pricing decisions. If the cross-elasticity in response to the price of substitutes is greater than 1, it would not be advisable to increase the price. Reducing the price, instead may prove beneficial. If the price of the complementary good is rising, it would be beneficial to reduce the price of the commodity.

3.3 Determinants of Price-elasticity of demand

The price-elasticity of demand varies between zero and infinity ($0 \leq e_p \leq \infty$). The price-elasticity of demand for a product within this range will depend on the following factors:

1. *Availability of Substitutes for the product*. This is one of the most important determinants of the price-elasticity of demand for a product. The higher the degree of closeness between the commodity and its substitutes, the greater the price-elasticity of demand for the commodity.

2. *Nature of the Commodity*. Commodities can be grouped as luxuries, comforts, and necessities. The demand for luxury goods is more price-elastic than the demand for necessities and comforts. This is so because the consumption of luxury goods can be dispensed with or postponed when their prices rise. On the other hand, the consumption of necessities cannot be postponed and hence, their demand is price-inelastic. Comforts have more elastic demand than necessities, and less elastic demand than luxuries.

3. *Weightage in the Total Consumption*. The proportion of income which consumers spend on a particular commodity influences the elasticity of demand for such commodity. The larger the proportion of income spent on a commodity, the greater will be the elasticity of demand for such commodity, and *vice versa*.

4. *Time factor in adjustment of Consumption pattern*. Price-elasticity of demand depends on the time consumers need to adjust their consumption pattern to a new price. The longer the adjustment time, the greater the price-elasticity of demand

5. *Range of Commodity Use*. The range of uses of a given commodity can affect the elasticity of demand for such commodity. The wider the range of use of a product, the higher the elasticity of demand for such product. Electricity, for example, has a wide range of use including, lighting, cooking, and industrial activities. The demand for electricity therefore has greater elasticity.

3.4 Measuring Price-Elasticity of Demand from a Demand Function.

The price-elasticity of demand for a product can be measured directly from the demand function. We look at this from the perspective of the Linear demand function, as well as the non-linear demand function.

(i) Price-Elasticity from a Linear Demand Function. For a given linear demand function, you can measure the price-elasticity by first taking the first derivative with respect to the price variable, P, (dQ/dP), if price is the independent variable, or with respect to the quantity variable, Q, (dP/dQ), if quantity is the independent variable. The result will the be multiplied by the price-quantity ratio (P/Q) for the first case, and the quantity-price ratio (Q/P) for the second case. Consider a linear demand function:

$$Q = 210 - 0.1P,$$

the point elasticity can be measured for any price by using:

$$\frac{dQ}{dP} \cdot \frac{P}{Q} \qquad (3.4.1)$$

For P = N5/unit, the price-elasticity would be:

$-0.1(P/Q)$, since $\frac{d(210 - 0.1P)}{dP} = -0.1$

Given that P = 5 (as specified above), we solve for Q in the demand function to get:

$$Q = 210 - 0.1(5) = 210 - 0.5 = 209.5$$

Therefore, the required price-elasticity of demand becomes,

$e_p = -0.1(5/209.5) = -0.002.$

(ii) Price-Elasticity from a Non-Linear Demand Function. The computation of price-elasticity from a non-linear demand function follows the same process as that of the linear demand function. The only difference is in the nature of the demand function. If a non-linear demand function is given by:

$$Q = aP^{-b},$$

then, $e_p = \frac{dQ}{dP} \cdot \frac{P}{Q}$

where $\frac{dQ}{dP} = -baP^{-b-1}$

The price-elasticity of demand can therefore be expressed as:

$$e_p = -baP^{-b-1}(P/Q)$$

$$= \frac{-baP^{-b}}{Q}$$

Since $Q = aP^{-b}$, by substitution, you get:

$$ep = \frac{-baP^{-b}}{aP^{-b}} = -b \qquad (3.4.2)$$

According to equation (3.4.2), when a demand function is of a multiplicative or power form, the price-elasticity coefficient equals the power of the variable P. This implies that price-elasticity for multiplicative demand function remains constant, regardless of a change in the commodity price.

3.5 Self-Assessment Exercise

Define the own-price and cross-price elasticities of demand and explain how one differs from the other

4.0 Conclusion

This unit points out the importance of measuring price-elasticies of demand. It began by defining, with simple examples, own-price elasticity of demand and cross-price elasticity of demand. Other information you can gather from the unit are (i) the determinants of price-elasticity of demand; and, (ii) how to measure price-elasticity of demand from the demand function.

5.0 Summary

The own-price elasticity of demand is generally defined as the degree of responsiveness of demand for a commodity to changes in its own price. More precisely, it is the percentage change in quantity demanded as a result of *one* percent change in the price of the commodity. The own-price elasticity can be measured between two points on a demand curve (for ***arc elasticity***) or on a point (for ***point elasticity***).

The cross-elasticity (or cross-price elasticity) can be defined as the degree of responsiveness of demand for a commodity to the changes in price of its substitutes and complementary goods. The cross-elasticity of demand can be used to identify substitute and complementary goods for a given commodity. If the cross-price elasticity between two goods is positive, the two goods may be considered as substitutes to one another. The greater the cross-price elasticity coefficient, the closer the substitute. Similarly, if the cross-price elasticity is negative, the two goods may be considered as complements. The higher the negative cross-elasticity coefficient, the higher the degree of complementarity.

The determinants of a commodity's price-elasticity of demand include: availability of substitutes; nature of the commodity; weightage of the total consumption; time factor in adjustment of consumption pattern; and, range of commodity use.

6.0 Tutor-Marked Assignment
Suppose the demand function for a product is given by:
Qd = 500 – 5P, compute the:
- (d) quantity demanded at the unit price of N10
- (e) price to sell 200 units
- (f) price for zero demand
- (g) quantity demanded at zero price
- (h) the own-price elasticity of demand at the price for which 200 units are sold..

7.0 References
Dwivedi, D. N. (2002) *Managerial Economics, sixth edition* (New Delhi: Vikas Publishing House Ltd).

UNIT 11: PRICE ELASTICITY, REVENUES, AND INCOME ELASTICITY OF DEMAND

Content

1.0 Introduction
2.0 Objectives
3.0 Relationships Between Price elasticity, Revenues, and Income Elasticity of Demand
3.1 Price-Elasticity and Total Revenue
3.2 Income-Elasticity of Demand
3.3 Advertisement- or Promotional-Elasticity of Sales
3.4 Elasticity of Price-Expectations
3.5 Self-Assessment Exercise
4.0 Conclusion
5.0 Summary
6.0 Tutor-Marked Assignment
7.0 References

1.0 Introduction
This unit examines some important applications of price-elaticity of demand, especially in the areas of total revenue and marginal revenue from the sale of goods and services. It also extends the discussions of elasticity to those of income, advertisement, and price expectations.

2.0 Objectives
By the end of this unit, you should be able to:
1. Expand your understanding of elasticity of demand
2. Know how demand elasticity, revenue, and income are related
3. Apply the concept of demand elasticity to sales forecasts and planning.

3.0 Relationships Between Price elasticity, Revenues, and Income Elasticity of Demand

3.1 Price-Elasticity and Total Revenue
A revenue-maximising firm would be interested in knowing whether increasing or decreasing the commodity price would maximise revenue. The price-elasticity of demand for the firm's product at different price levels would provide the answer this question. The answer would come from the fact that if $e_p > 1$, then decreasing the price will increase the total revenue, and if $e_p < 1$, then increasing the price will increase the total revenue.

The relationship between price-elasticity (e_p) and total revenue (TR) is sumarised in table 3.1.1 below.

Table 3.1.1: Price-Elasticity, Price-Change, and Change in Total Revenue

Elasticity Coefficient	If Price:	Then Total Revenue Will:
$e_p = 0$	Increases	Increase

		Decreases	Decrease
$e_p < 1$		Increases	Increase
		Decreases	Decrease
$e_p = 1$		Increase	No change
		Decrease	No change
$e_p > 1$		Increase	Decrease
		Decrease	Increase
$e_p = \infty$		Increase	Decrease to zero
		Decrease	Infinite increase, depending on size of the market

3.1.1 Price-Elasticity and Marginal Revenue

Note that Marginal Revenue (MR) is the first derivative of the total revenue (TR) function, and that TR = PQ (P = unit price; Q = quantity sold). The relationship between price-elasticity, MR, and TR is shown by the following derivations:

Since TR = P.Q,

$$MR = \frac{d(P.Q)}{dQ} = P + Q\frac{dP}{dQ} \quad \text{(the product rule of differentiation)}$$

$$= P\left[1 + \frac{Q}{P} \cdot \frac{dQ}{dQ}\right] \quad (3.1.1)$$

Note that in equation (3.3.7.3)::

$$\frac{Q}{P} \cdot \frac{dQ}{dP} = -1/e_p$$

By substituting $-1/e_p$ into equation (3.1.1), you get:

$$MR = P[1 - 1/e_p] \quad (3.1.2)$$

Given this relationship between Marginal Revenue (MR) and price-elasticity of demand (e_p), the deciding manager can easily know whether it will be beneficial to change the price.

From equation (3.1.2), you can deduce that if $e_p = 1$, MR = 0. It follows that change in price will not affect the total revenue (TR).

If $e_p < 1$, MR < 0, TR decreases when price decreases, and TR increases when price increases. And if $e_p > 1$, MR > 0, TR increases when price decreases, and *vice versa*.

3.2: Income-Elasticity of Demand

The income-elasticity of demand can be defined as the degree of responsiveness of demand to changes in the consumer's income. Note that unlike the price-elasticity of demand, which is always negative due to the negative slope of the demand function, the income-elasticity of demand is always positive. This is because of the positive relationship between demand and the consumer's income. This is the case however, for normal goods. In the case of inferior goods, the income-elasticity of demand is always negative. This is so because the demand for inferior goods decreases with increases in consumer's income, and vice versa.

The income-elasticity of demand for a commodity, say X can be computed by:
$$e_y = \frac{Y}{Q_x} \cdot \frac{\Delta Q_x}{\Delta Y} \quad (3.2.1)$$
Where, e_y = income-elasticity of demand; Y = consumer's income; Qx = quantity demanded of commodity X.

As noted above, for all normal goods, the income-elasticity is positive. However, the degree or magnitude of elasticity varies in accordance with the nature and type of commodities. Consumer goods of the three categories: *necessities, comforts*, and *luxuries* have different elastiticies. The general pattern of income-elasticities of different kinds of goods for increase in income and their effects on sales is given in table 3.2.1 below for managers to take note:

Table 3.2.1: Magnitude of Income-Elasticity for different Categories of Goods

Consumer Goods	Coefficient of Income-Elasticity	Effect on Sales
Essential Goods	Less than 1 or unity ($e_y < 1$)	Less than proportionate change in sales
Comforts	Almost equal to unity ($e_y \equiv 1$)	Almost proportionate change in sales
Luxuries	Greater than unity ($e_y > 1$)	More than proportionate increase in sales

Own-price and cross-elasticities of demand are specifically significant in the pricing of products aimed at the maximisation of short-run revenues. Income-elasticity of products is highly significant in long-run planning and management of production, especially during the period of business cycles.

The concept of income-elasticity can be used in the estimation of future demand, provided that the rate of increase in income and income-elasticity of demand for the given product are known. This can be useful in forecasting demand for expected changes in consumers' personal incomes, other things remaining the same. Knowledge of income-elasticity of demand is also helpful in the avoidance of over- and under-production.

3.3 Advertisement- or Promotional-Elasticity of Sales

It is a known fact that expenditure on advertisements and on other sales promotion activities help in promoting sales, but not in the same magnitude or degree at all levels of sales. The concept of advertisement elasticity is found useful in the determination of optimum level of advertisement expenditure. This concept assumes a greater significance in deciding advertisement expenditure than other decision variables. This is so especially when the government imposes restriction on advertisement cost (as is the case in most developed economies), or there is competitive advertising by the rival firms.

By definition, advertisement-elasticity of sales is the degree of responsiveness of sales to changes in advertisement expenditures. It can be computed by the formula:

$$e_A = \frac{\Delta S}{\Delta A} \cdot \frac{A}{S} \qquad (3.3.1)$$

where S = sales; ΔS = change in sales; A = initial advertisement cost; and, ΔA = additional expenditure on advertisement

The advertisement-elasticity of sales varies between zero and infinity. Thus,

$$0 \leq e_A \leq \infty$$

Some values of the advertisement-elasticity of sales can be interpreted according to table 3.3.1 below:

Table 3.3.1: Interpretation of Advertisement-Elasticity of Sales

Elasticity (e_A)	Interpretation
$e_A = 0$	Sales do not respond to advertisement expenditure
$0 < e_A < 1$	Increase in total Sales is less than proportionate to the increase in advertisement expenditure
$e_A = 1$	Sales increase in proportion to the increase in expenditure on advertisement
$e_A > 1$	Sales increase at a higher rate than the rate of increase in advertisement expenditure.

Some of the *important factors affecting the advertisement-elasticity* of sales can be outlined as follows:

(i) *The level of total sales*. As sales increase, the advertisement-elasticity of sales decreases.

(ii) *Advertisement by rival firms*. In a highly competitive market, the effectiveness of advertisement by a firm is determined by the relative effectiveness of advertisement by the rival firms

(iii) *Cumulative effect of past advertisements*. Additional doses of advertisement expenditures do have cumulative effect on the promotion of sales, and this may considerably increase the advertisement-elasticity of sales.

Other factors affecting the advertisement-elasticity of sales are those factors demand for the product, including *change in product's price; consumer's income; growth of substitute goods and their prices.*

3.4 Elasticity of Price-Expectations
During the period of price fluctuations, consumer's price expectations play a significant role in determining demand for a given commodity. The price-expectation-elasticity refers to the expected change in future price as a result of changes in current prices of a given product. The elasticity of price-expectation is defined and measured by the following formula:

$$e_x = \frac{\Delta P_f}{\Delta P_c} \cdot \frac{P_c}{P_f} \qquad (3.4.1)$$

where P_c and P_f are *current* and *future* prices, respectively.

The coefficient e_x is a measure of expected percentage change in future price due to a 1 percent change in current price. $e_x > 1$ implies that future change in price will be greater than the current change in price, and *vice versa*. $e_x = 1$ implies that the future change in price will be equal to the change in current price.

The concept of elasticity of price-expectation is very useful in future pricing policies. For instance, if $e_x > 1$, sellers will be able to sell more in the future at higher prices. Accordingly, businesspeople may determine their future pricing policies.

3.5 Self-Assessment Exercise
What are the possible consequences of a large-scale firm placing its product in the market without having estimated the demand for its product?

4.0 Conclusion
This unit has exposed you further to the concepts and applications of elasticity of demand. You have observed the important relationship between price elasticity of demand and revenue, and the relationship between price elasticity of demand and marginal revenue. These relationships will help you in your pricing decisions, especially when your business objective is to maximise sales revenue.

You also learned that consumers' price expectations play significant roles in determining the demand for your commodity. This is especially the case for periods of general price fluctuations.

5.0 Summary
The points made by this unit can be summarised by you as follows:
1. A revenue-maximising firm would be interested in knowing whether increasing or decreasing the commodity price would maximise revenue. The price-elasticity of

demand for the firm's product at different price levels would provide the answer this question. The answer would come from the fact that if $e_p > 1$, then decreasing the price will increase the total revenue, and if $e_p < 1$, then increasing the price will increase the total revenue.

2. The income-elasticity of demand can be defined as the degree of responsiveness of demand to changes in the consumer's income. The income-elasticity of demand is always positive, especially for normal goods. In the case of inferior goods, the income-elasticity of demand is always negative. This is so because the demand for inferior goods decreases with increases in consumer's income, and vice versa.

3. The concept of advertisement elasticity is found useful in the determination of optimum level of advertisement expenditure. This concept assumes a greater significance in deciding advertisement expenditure than other decision variables.

4. During the period of price fluctuations, consumer's price expectations play a significant role in determining demand for a given commodity. The price-expectation-elasticity refers to the expected change in future price as a result of changes in current prices of a given product.

6.0 Tutor-Marked Assignment

Given the demand function:

$Q_d = 12 - P$

(a) Using some hypothetical figures for Q_d and P, present the demand and marginal revenue (MR) schedules
(b) Plot the average revenue (AR) and MR schedules
(c) Find the marginal revenue when P = 12, 10, 6, and 4
(d) Estimate the elasticity coefficient of the demand curve, when the total revenue is at its maximum.

7.0 References

Dwivedi, D. N. (2002) *Managerial Economics, sixth edition* (New Delhi: Vikas Publishing House Ltd).

UNIT 12: DEMAND FORECASTING

Content
1.0 Introduction

2.0 Objectives
3.0 Demand Forecasting
3.1 Demand Forecasting Techniques
3.2 Self-Assessment Exercise
4.0 Conclusion
5.0 Summary
6.0 Tutor-Marked Assignment
7.0 References

1.0 Introduction

The term demand forecasting in our context simply means predicting the future demand for a product. Information regarding future demand is essential for scheduling and planning production, acquisition of raw materials, acquisition of finance, and advertising. Forecasting is most useful where large-scale production is involved and production requires long gestation period.

2.0 Objectives

When you go through this unit, you will be able to:
1. Know about how to forecast demand for your products
2. Have at your finger tips the latest forecasting techniques
3. Formulate models that can aid you in forecasting demand

3.0 Demand Forecasting

3.1 Demand Forecasting Techniques

There are many techniques employed in demand forecasting, but of most important in our discussions are the *Survey* and *Statistical* methods.

3.1.1 The Survey Techniques

Survey techniques are used where the purpose is to make short-run demand forecasts. This technique uses consumer surveys to collect information about their intentions and future purchase plans. It involves:

(i) survey of potential consumers to elicit information on their intentions and plans;

(ii) opinion polling of experts, that is, opinion survey of market experts and sales representatives;

The methods used in conducting the survey of consumers and experts include:

Consumer Survey Methods (direct interviews). Direct interview of the potential consumers may be in the form of:

(a) *Complete Enumeration.* In this case, almost all the consumers or users of the product in question are contacted to ascertain their future of purchasing the product. The quantities indicated by the consumers are added together to obtain the probable demand for the product. If, for example, a majority of n out of m households in a given geographical location indicate the quantity, (q) they will be willing to purchase of a commodity, then the total probable demand (D_p) may be obtained as:

$$D_p = q_1 + q_2 + q_3 + \ldots + q_n$$

where $q_1, q_2, q_3, \ldots n$, represent demand by individual households.

This method can, however, be useful for products whose consumers are concentrated in a certain locality. It may not be physically possible for cases where the market is widely dispersed.

(b) *Sample Survey.* In a sample survey, only few potential consumers and users of the products are selected as respondents from the relevant market. The survey may take the form of either direct interview or mailed questionnaire to the sample consumers. On the basis of information obtained thereof, the probable demand (D_p) can be estimated by the simple formula:

$$D_p = \frac{H_R}{H_S} (H, A_D)$$

where H_R = number of households indicating demand for the product
H_S = the number of households surveyed
H = the census number of households from the relevant market.
A_D = average expected demand as indicated by the households
survey = total quantity of demand indicated ÷ number of households.

Though this method is widely used for forecasting demand, it has limitations similar to those of the complete enumeration method.

(c) *The End-Use Method.* This method of forecasting demand has a considerable theoretical and practical importance, especially in ***forecasting demand for inputs***. The method involves four basic stages:

Stage 1: This stage requires that all the possible users of the product in question be identified and listed.

Stage 2: The second stage involves fixing suitable technical norms of consumption, expressed in either per unit of production of the complete product or, in some cases, per unit of investment or per capita use.

Stage 3: Having established the technical norms of consumption for the different industries and other end uses of the product, the third step is the application of the norms. This requires the knowledge of the desired or targeted levels of output of the individual industries for the reference year, and also the likely development in other economic activities for which the product is used.

Stage 4: The final stage in the end-use method of demand forecasting involves the aggregation of the product-wise or use-wise content of the item for which the demand is to be forecast. Result of this aggregation gives the estimate of demand for the product as a whole for the terminal year in question.

Opinion Poll Methods. These methods aim at collecting opinions of those possessing knowledge of the market, such as the sales representatives, sales executives, professional marketing experts, and marketing consultants. The opinion poll methods include:
 (a) The Expert-Opinion method;
 (b) Delphi method; and,
 (c) Market Studies and Experiments

The Expert-Opinion Method. This method involves the use of sales representatives in the assessment of demand for the product in the areas, States or cities they represent. The sales representatives are expected to know the future purchasing plans of consumers they transact business with. The estimates of demand thus obtained from the different sales representatives at different areas, States and cities are added up to get the overall probable demand for the product in question.

The Delphi Method. This method of demand forecasting is an extension of the simple expert opinion poll method. It is used to consolidate the divergent expert opinions and to arrive at a compromise estimate of future demand.

In the Delphi method, the experts are provided with some information on estimates of forecasts of other experts, along with the underlying assumptions. It will then be the consensus of the experts about the forecasts that will become the final forecast for the future demand.

Market Studies and Experiments. This method requires that firms first select some areas of representative markets, about four cities with similar features in terms of population, income level, cultural and social background, occupational distribution, and consumer preferences and choices. This is followed by market experiments involving changing prices, advertisement expenditures, and other controllable variables in the demand function, all things being equal. These variables are changed over time, either simultaneously in all the markets or in selected markets. Having introduced these changes, the consequent changes in demand over a period of time are then recorded. Based on these data, elasticity coefficients are then computed, and these coefficients are used to assess the forecast demand for the product.

3.1.2. Statistical Techniques
The statistical techniques of demand forecasting use historical (or time-series), and cross-section data for estimating long-term demand for a product. The techniques are found more reliable than those of the survey techniques. They include: (i) the Trend Projection techniques; (ii) the Barometric techniques; and, (iii) the Econometric techniques. Our discussions will, however, concentrate on the Econometric techniques as these are more superior and reliable than the Trend Projection and Barometric techniques.

The Econometric Techniques.
The Econometric techniques include: (i) Regression method; and, (ii) Simultaneous Equation method.

3.1.3 The Regression Method.
Regression analysis is found to be the most popular method of demand estimation and/or forecasting. It combines economic theory and statistical techniques of estimation. The economic theory specifies the determinants of demand and the nature of the relationship between the demand for a product and its determinants. It helps in ascertaining the general form of demand function. Statistical techniques on the other hand are employed in estimating the values of the parameters in the estimated equation.

In regression models, the quantity to be forecast in the demand function is the *dependent* variable, and the determinants of demand are the *independent* or *explanatory* variables.

In specifying the demand functions for various commodities, the forecaster may come across many commodities whose demand depends, at large, on a single independent variable. For instance, suppose the demand for sugar in a given geographical area is found to depend largely on the population, then the demand function for sugar will be referred to as a *single-variable* demand function. But if it is found that demand functions for fruits and vegetables depend on a number of variables such as, their own-prices, substitutes, household income, population, and the like, then such demand functions are referred to as *multi-variable* demand functions. The single regression equation is used for single-variable demand functions, while the multi-variable equation is used for multi-variable demand functions. The single-variable and multi-variable regressions are outlined below.

The Simple or Bivariate Regression Technique
As mentioned earlier, in a simple regression technique, a single independent variable is used in estimating the statistical value of the dependent variable or the variable to be forecast. This technique is similar to trend fitting, though, in trend fitting, the independent variable is time, t, while in the case of simple regression, the chosen independent variable is the single most important determinant of demand.

Suppose we want to forecast the demand for sugar, for example, for particular periods on the basis of some past data, we would estimate the regression equation of the form:

$$Y = a + bX \qquad (3.1.1)$$

where Y represents the quantity of sugar to be demanded; and, X represents the single variable, population, and a and b are constants.

The parameters a and b can be estimated, using the past data, by solving the following corresponding linear quations for a and b:

$$\sum Y_i = na + b\sum X_i \qquad (3.1.2)$$
$$\sum X_i Y_i = a\sum X_i + bX_i^2 \qquad (3.1.3)$$

The procedures for calculating the terms in equations (3.1.2) and (3.1.3) can be illustrated by the following example. Consider the following hypothetical past data on the demand for sugar for the years 2000 to 2006:

Table 3.1.1: Demand for Sugar

Year	Population (millions)	Quantity of sugar demanded (000's)
2000	10	40
2001	12	50
2002	15	60
2003	20	70
2004	25	80
2005	30	90
2006	40	100

Using this hypothetical data, we can calculate the terms as shown in table 3.1.2 below:

Table 3.1.2: Calculation of Terms of the Linear Equations in Simple Regression

Year	Population (X_i)	Quantity of sugar (Y_i)	X_i^2	$X_i Y_i$
2000	10	40	100	400
2001	12	50	144	600
2002	15	60	225	900
2003	20	70	400	1400
2004	25	80	625	2000
2005	30	90	900	2700
2006	40	100	1600	4000
n=7	$\sum X_i = 152$	$\sum Y_i = 490$	$\sum X^2 = 3994$	$\sum X_i Y_i = 12000$

Substituting the related values from table 3.1.2 into equations (3..1.2) and (3.1.3), we get:

$$490 = 7a + 152b \qquad (3.1.4)$$
$$12000 = 152a + 3994b \qquad (3.1.5)$$

Solving simultaneously for a and b in the above equations, we obtain:
  a = 27.44; b = 1.96. substituting these values into the regression equation (3.3.11), the estimated regression equation becomes:

$$\hat{Y} = 27.44 + 1.96X \qquad (3.1.6)$$

With the regression equation (3.1.6), the demand for the commodity concerned can be easily forecast for any period provided that the figure for the population or any single determinant of demand is known. Suppose the population for the year 2008 is projected to be 100 million then the demand for sugar, according to our example, would be estimated using the regression equation as:

Y = 27.44 + 1.96(100) = 27.44 + 1960 = 223,440 units.

The simple regression technique is based on the following assumptions:
4. the independent variable will continue to grow at the estimated growth rate, 1.96 according to regression equation (3.1.6);
5. the relationship between the dependent and independent variables will continue to remain the same in the future as in the past.

The Multi-Variate Regression Technique
The technique is used in cases where the demand for a commodity is determined to be a function of many independent variables, or where the explanatory variables are greater than one. The analysis in this technique is referred to as multiple regression analysis.

The procedure of multiple regression analysis involves the following steps:

Step One: *Specification of the independent or explanatory variables*, that is, the variables that explain the variations in demand for the commodity in question. These variables are identified from the determinants of demand as listed earlier.

Step Two: *Collection of time-series data on the independent variable*. Here, the necessary data on both the dependent (the demand for the commodity) and independent variables (the determinants of demand) are collected.

Step Three: *Specification of the Regression Equation*. The reliability of the demand forecast depends to a large extent on the form of regression equation and the degree of consistency of the explanatory variables in the estimated demand function. The greater the degree of consistency, the higher will be the reliability of the estimated demand function and *vice versa*.

The final step is to employ the necessary statistical technique in estimating the parameters of the regression equation. Some common forms of multi-variate demand functions are as follows:

1. The Linear Function. The linear demand function is where the relationship between the demand and its determinants is formulated by a straight line. The most common type of this equation is of the form:

$$Q_x = \alpha - bP_x + cY + dP_s + JA \qquad (3.1.7)$$

where Q_x = quantity demanded of commodity X; P_x = unit price of commodity X; Y = consumer's income; P_s = price of substitute good; A = advertisement expenditure; α is a constant (or the demand intercept), and b, c, d, and j are the parameters (or regression coefficients) expressing the relationship between demand and P_x, Y, P_s, and A, respectively.

In linear demand functions, quantity demanded is assumed to change with changes in independent variables at a constant rate. The parameters are estimated by using the least-squares method. Having estimated the parameters, the demand can be easily forecast if data on the independent variables for the reference period are available.

2. The Power Function. In the linear functions of demand, the marginal effects on demand of independent variables are assumed to be constant and independent of changes in other variables. It is assumed, for instance, that the marginal effect of a change in own price is independent of change in income or other independent variables. There may, however, be cases in which it is intuitively or theoretically found that the marginal effect of the independent variables on demand is neither constant nor independent of the values of all other variables included in the demand function. For example, the effect of an increase in the price of sugar on demand may be neutralised by a rise in consumer's income. In such cases, a multiplicative or 'power' form of the demand function, considered to be the most logical form, is used for estimating the demand of a commodity. The power form of the demand function is given by:

$$Q_x = \alpha P_x^b Y^c P_s \, A \qquad (3.1.8)$$

The algebraic form of multiplicative demand function can be transformed into a log-linear form for simplicity in estimation as follows:

$$\text{Log } Q_x = \log \alpha - b \log P_x + c \log Y + d \log P_s + j \log A \qquad (3.1.9)$$

This can be estimated using the least-squares regression technique. The estimated function can easily be used in forecasting the future demand for the given commodity.

3.1.4 The Simultaneous Equations Method
This method of demand forecasting involves the estimation of several simultaneous equations. These equations are, generally, behavioural equations, mathematical identities, and market-clearing equations. Demand forecasting using econometric models of simultaneous equations enables the forecaster take into account the simultaneous interaction between dependent and independent variables.

The simultaneous equations method is a complete and systematic approach to forecasting in general. It uses sophisticated mathematical and statistical tools which are beyond the scope of the present discussions. In effect, our discussions here will be restricted to the basic steps in the application of this method of forecasting.

The *first step* is to develop a complete model and specify the behavioural assumptions regarding the variables included in the model. The variables included in the model are referred to as (i) endogenous variables, and (ii) exogenous variables.

The *endogenous variables* are variables whose values are determined within the model. Endogenous variables are included in the model as dependent variables or variables to be explained by the model. These variables are often referred to in econometrics as 'controlled' variables. Note that *the number of equations in the model must equal the number of endogenous variables*.

Exogenous variables are those whose values are determined outside the model. They are referred to as inputs of the model. The purpose of a given model will determine whether a variable is endogenous or exogenous. Exogenous variables are also looked at as 'uncontrolled variables.

The *second step* is to collect the necessary data on both endogenous and exogenous variables. If you find that data is not available, they can be generated from available primary or secondary sources.

Having developed the model, and the necessary data collected, the *third step* is to estimate the model using the appropriate method, and the *two-stage least-squares* method to predict the values of the exogenous variables.

Finally, the model is solved for each endogenous variable in terms of exogenous variables. By plugging the values of exogenous variables into the equations, the objective value can be calculated and prediction made.

The simultaneous equation method is theoretically superior to the simple regression method. The main advantage of the method is that it is capable of capturing the influence of dependency of the variables. The major limitation is non-availability of adequate data.

The following example illustrates the simultaneous equation method. A simple macroeconomic model is given below:

$$Y_t = C_t + I_t + G_t + X_t \qquad (3.1.10)$$

where,
Y_t = Gross National Product (GNP)
C_t = Total consumption expenditure
I_t = Gross Private Investment
G_t = Government expenditure
X_t = Net Export (X – M), where X represents Export, and M, Import.
Subscript t represents a given time unit.

Equation (3.3.20) is an identity that can be explained with a system of simultaneous equations, such as:

$$C_t = a + bY_t \quad (3.1.11)$$
$$I_t = 20 \quad (3.1.12)$$
$$G_t = 10 \quad (3.1.13)$$
$$X_t = 5 \quad (3.1.14)$$

In the above system of equations, Y_t and C_t are the endogenous variables, and I_t, G_t, and X_t, are exogenous variables. Equation (3.1.11) is a regression equation that needs to be estimated. Equations (3.1.12) to (3.1.1) show the values of exogenous variables determined outside the model.

Suppose you want to predict the values of Y_t and C_t simultaneously, and that when you estimated equation (3.1.11) you get:

$$C_t = 100 + 0.75Y_t \quad (3.1.15)$$

Using this equation, the value of Yt can be determined as:

$$Y_t = C_t + I_t + G_t + X_t$$

$$= 100 + 0.75Y_t + 20 + 10 + 5 = 0.75Y_t + 135$$

$$Y_t - 0.75Y_t = 135$$

$$0.25Y_t = 135$$
$$Y_t = 135/0.25 = 540.$$

Using this value of Y_t, you can evaluate the value of C_t as follows:

$$C_t = 100 + 0.75Y_t$$

$$= 100 + 0.75(540) = 100 + 405 = 505.$$

It follows that the predicted values will be:

$$Y_t = 540$$
$$C_t = 505$$
$$Y_t = 505 + 20 + 10 + 5 = 540.$$

Note that the above example of econometric model is an extremely simplified model. In actual practice, the econometric models are generally very complex.

3.2 Self-Assessment Exercise
Discuss the necessary steps in the application of the simultaneous equation method of forecasting

4.0 Conclusion

You must have learned some useful forecasting techniques from this unit. You also learned that the term demand forecasting simply means predicting the future demand for a product. Information regarding future demand is essential for scheduling and planning production, acquisition of raw materials, acquisition of finance, and advertising. Forecasting is most useful where large-scale production is involved and production requires long gestation period.

5.0 Summary

Among the numerous techniques employed in demand forecasting, the most important of them are the *Survey* and *Statistical* techniques. The survey techniques are used where the purpose is to make short-run demand forecasts. This technique uses consumer surveys to collect information about their intentions and future purchase plans. It involves:
(i) survey of potential consumers to elicit information on their intentions and plans; and,
(ii) opinion polling of experts, that is, opinion survey of market experts and sales representatives.

The statistical techniques use historical (or time-series), and cross-section data for estimating long-term demand for a product. The techniques are found more reliable than those of the survey techniques. They include: (i) the Trend Projection techniques; (ii) the Barometric techniques; and, (iii) the Econometric techniques. Our discussions, however, concentrated on the Econometric techniques as these are more superior and reliable than the Trend Projection and Barometric techniques.

6.0 Tutor-Marked Assignment

An Economic Research Centre has published data on the Gross Domestic Product (GDP) and the Demand for refrigerators as presented below:

Year:	2000	2001	2002	2003	2004	2005	2006
GDP (N' billions):	20	22	25	27	30	33	35
Refrigerators (millions):	5	6	8	8	9	10	12

(a) Estimate the regression equation, $R = a + bY$
where R = refrigerators (in millions), and Y = GDP (in N'billions)
(b) Forecast the demand for refrigerators for the years 2007, 2008, and 2009, if the Research Centre projected the GDP for 2007, 2008, and 2009 to be N40 billion, N52 billion, and N65 billion, respectively

7.0 References

1. Dwivedi, D. N. (2002) *Managerial Economics, sixth edition* (New Delhi: Vikas Publishing House Ltd).

2. Haessuler, E. F. and Paul, R. S. (1976), *Introductory Mathematical Analysis for Students of Business and Economics, 2nd edition* (Reston Virginia: Reston Publishing Company)

UNIT 13: THE THEORY OF PRODUCTION

Content
1.0 Introduction
2.0 Objectives

3.0 The Theory of Production
3.1 The Production Function
3.2 Self-Assessment Exercise
4.0 Conclusion
5.0 Summary
6.0 Tutor-Marked Assignment
7.0 References

1.0 Introduction
No matter the objective of any business organisation, achievement of efficiency in production or cost minimisation for a given production activity appear to be one of the prime concern of the managers. As a matter of fact, the survival of a business firm in a competitive environment depends on its ability to produce at competitive costs. Firms are, therefore, mandated to either minimise costs of production or maximise output from a given quantity of inputs. In the manager's effort to minimise production costs, the fundamental questions he or she faces are:
   (f) How can production be optimized or costs minimised?
   (g) What will be the beaviour of output as inputs increase?
   (h) How does technology help in reducing production costs?
   (i) How can the least-cost combination of inputs be achieved?
   (j) Given the technology, what happens to the rate of return when more plants are added to the firm?

The theory of production attempts to provide theoretical answers to these questions, through abstract models built under hypothetical conditions. It follows that, though production theories may not provide solutions to the real life business problems, it can provide tools and techniques for the analysis of production conditions and for finding solutions to the practical business problems.

In this unit, we present the theory of production. In unit 14, the discussions will be extended to other important aspects of production, including economies of scale and optimal input combinations.

2.0 Objectives
At the end of this unit, should be able to:
1. Understand the relationships between production and the factors of production
2. Provide answers to the fundamental questions managers ask themselves in their efforts to minimise costs of production.
3. Understand the basic forms of production functions
4. Make efficient production decisions

3.0 The Theory of Production
Production theory generally deals with quantitative relationships, that is, technical and technological relationships between inputs, especially labour and capital, and between inputs and outputs.

An *input* is a good or service that goes into the production process. As economists refer to it, an input is simply anything which a firm buys for use in its production process. An *output*, on the other hand, is any good or service that comes out of a production process.

Economists classified inputs as (i) labour; (ii) capital; (iii) land; (iv) raw materials; and, (v) time. These variables are measured per unit of time and hence referred to as flow variables. In recent times, entrepreneurship has been added as part of the production inputs, though this can be measured by the managerial expertise and the ability to make things happen.

Inputs are classified as either *fixed* or *variable* inputs. Fixed and variable inputs are defined in both economic sense and technical sense. In *economic sense,* a fixed input is one whose supply is inelastic in the short run. In *technical sense*, a fixed input is one that remains fixed (or constant) for certain level of output.

A variable input is one whose supply in the short run is elastic, example, labour, raw materials, and the like. Users of such inputs can employ a larger quantity in the short run. Technically, a variable input is one that changes with changes in output. In the long run, all inputs are variable.

3.1 The Production Function

Production function is a tool of analysis used in explaining the input-output relationship. It describes the technical relationship between inputs and output in physical terms. In its general form, it holds that production of a given commodity depends on certain specific inputs. In its specific form, it presents the quantitative relationships between inputs and outputs. A production function may take the form of a schedule, a graph line or a curve, an algebraic equation or a mathematical model. The production function represents the technology of a firm.

An empirical production function is generally so complex to include a wide range of inputs: land, labour, capital, raw materials, time, and technology. These variables form the independent variables in a firm's actual production function. A firm's long-run production function is of the form:

$Q = f(L_d, L, K, M, T, t)$ (3.1.1)

where L_d = land and building; L = labour; K = capital; M = materials; T = technology; and, t = time.

For sake of convenience, economists have reduced the number of variables used in a production function to only two: capital (K) and labour (L). Therefore, in the analysis of input-output relations, the production function is expressed as:

$Q = f(K, L)$ (3.1.2)

Equation (3.1.2) represents the algebraic or mathematical form of the production function. It is this form of production function which is most commonly used in production analysis.

As implied by the production function (equation (3.1.2)), increasing production, Q, will require K and L, and whether the firm can increase both K and L or only L will depend on the time period it takes into account for increasing production, that is, whether the firm is thinking in terms of the *short run* or in terms of the *long run.*

Economists believe that the supply of capital (K) is *inelastic* in the short run and *elastic* in the long run. Thus, in the short run firms can increase production only by increasing labour, since the supply of capital is fixed in the short run. In the long run, the firm can employ more of both capital and labour, as the supply of capital becomes elastic over time. In effect, there exists two types of production functions:

The short-run production function; and,
The long-run production function

3.1.1 The Short- and Long-Run Production Functions
The *short-run* production function, often referred to as the *single variable production function*, can be written as:

$$Q = f(L) \tag{3.1.3}$$

In the *long-run*, both capital (K) and labour (L) is included in the production function, so that the long-run production function can be written as:

$$Q = f(K, L) \tag{3.1.4}$$

A production function *is based on the following assumptions*:
(i) perfect divisibility of both inputs and output;
(ii) there are only two factors of production – capital (K) and lacour (L);
(iii) limited substitution of one factor for the other;
(iv) a given technology; and,
(v) inelastic supply of fixed factors in the short-run.

Any changes in the above assumptions would require modifications in the production function.

The two most important forms of production functions used in economic literature in analysing input-output relationships are the *Cobb-Douglas* production function and the *Constant Elasticity of Substitution (CES)* production function. Our interest at this level will be limited to the Cobb-Douglas production function.

3.1.2 The Cobb-Douglas Production Function
The Cobb-Douglas production function is of the following general form:

$$Q = AK^aL^b \tag{3.1.5}$$

where a and b are positive fractions.

The Cobb-Douglas production function is often used in its following form:

$$Q = AK^aL^{(1-a)} \tag{3.1.6}$$

Properties of the Cobb-Douglas Production Function

A power function of the Cobb-Douglas type has the following important properties:

First, the multiplicative form of the power function (3.1.5) can be transformed into its log-linear form as:
$$\log Q = \log A + a \log K + b \log L \tag{3.1.7}$$

In its logarithmic form, the function becomes simple to handle and can be empirically estimated using linear regression techniques.

Second, power functions are homogeneous and the degree of homogeneity is given by the sum of the exponents a and b as in the Cobb-Douglas function. If a + b = 1, then the production function is homogeneous of degree 1 and implies constant returns to scale.

Third, a and b represent the elasticity coefficient of output for inputs, K and L, respectively. The output elasticity coefficient (ε) in respect of capital can be defined as proportional change in output as a result of a given change in K, keeping L constant. Thus,

$$\varepsilon_k = \frac{\partial Q/Q}{\partial K/K} = \frac{\partial Q}{\partial K} \cdot \frac{K}{Q} \tag{3.1.8}$$

By differentiating the production function, $Q = AK^aL^b$, with respect to K and substituting the result into equation (3.1.8), the elasticity coefficient, ε_k, can be derived:

$$\frac{\partial Q}{\partial K} = aAK^{(a-1)}L^b$$

Substituting the values for Q (equation (4.5)) and $\partial Q/\partial K$ into equation (3.1.8), you get:

$$\varepsilon_k = a AK^{(a-1)}L^b \left[\frac{K}{AK^aL^b} \right]$$
$$= a$$

It follows that the output coefficient for capital, K, is 'a'. The same procedure may be applied to show that 'b' is the elasticity coefficient of output for labour, L.

Fourth, the constants a and b represent the relative distributive share of inputs K and L in the total output, Q. The share of K in Q is given by:

$$\frac{\partial Q}{\partial K} \cdot K$$

Similarly, the share of L in Q can be obtained by:

$$\frac{\partial Q}{\partial L} \cdot L$$

The relative share of K in Q can be obtained as:

$$\frac{\partial Q}{\partial K} \cdot K \cdot \frac{1}{Q} = a$$

and the relative share of L in Q can be obtained as:

$$\frac{\partial Q}{\partial L} \cdot L \cdot \frac{1}{Q} = b$$

Finally, the Cobb-Douglas production function in its general form, $Q = K^a L^{(1-a)}$, implies that at zero cost, there will be zero production.

Some of the necessary concepts in production analysis can be easily derived from the Cobb-Douglas production function as shown below:

1. Average Products of L (AP_L) and K (AP_K):
   $AP_L = A (K/L)^{(1-a)}$
   $AP_K = A (L/K)^1$

2. Marginal Products of L (MP_L) and K (MP_K):
   $MP_L = a(Q/L)$
   $MP_K = (1 - a)Q/K$

3. Marginal Rate of Technical Substitution of L for K ($MRTS_{L,K}$):
   $$MRTS_{L,K} = \frac{MP_L}{MP_K} = \frac{a}{(1-a)} \cdot \frac{K}{L}$$

Note the $MRTS_{L,K}$ is the rate at which a marginal unit of labour, L, can be substituted for a marginal unit of capital, K (along a given isoquant) without affecting the total output.

3.2 Self-Assessment Exercise
How does Cobb-Douglas production function differ from the standard short-run production function?

4.0 Conclusion
This unit points out that production theory deals with quantitative relationships, otherwise known as technical and technological relationships between inputs, especially labour and capital, and between inputs and outputs.

An *input* has been defined as a good or service that goes into the production process. In economic terms, an input is simply anything which a firm buys for use in its production process. An *output*, on the other hand, is any good or service that comes out of a production process.

Economists classified inputs as (i) labour; (ii) capital; (iii) land; (iv) raw materials; and, (v) time. These variables are measured per unit of time and hence referred to as flow variables. In recent times, entrepreneurship has been added as part of the production inputs, though this can be measured by the managerial expertise and the ability to make things happen.

The unit discusses two major forms of production functions: (i) the short-and long-run production functions; and, (ii) the Cobb-Douglas production function.

5.0 Summary

The unit notes that production function is a tool of analysis used in explaining the input-output relationship. It describes the technical relationship between inputs and output in physical terms. It suggests that production of a given commodity depends on certain specific inputs. A production function may take the form of a schedule, a graph line or a curve, an algebraic equation or a mathematical model. The production function represents the technology of a firm.

An empirical production function is generally so complex to include a wide range of inputs: land, labour, capital, raw materials, time, and technology. These variables form the independent variables in a firm's actual production function. A firm's long-run production function is of the form:

A production function *is based on the following assumptions*:
(i) perfect divisibility of both inputs and output;
(ii) there are only two factors of production – capital (K) and lacour (L);
(iii) limited substitution of one factor for the other;
(iv) a given technology; and,
(v) inelastic supply of fixed factors in the short-run.

The two most important forms of production functions used in economic literature in analysing input-output relationships are the *Cobb-Douglas* production function and the *Constant Elasticity of Substitution (CES)* production function. The unit however, focused on the Cobb-Douglas form of production function. The Cobb-Douglas production function is of the following general form:

$Q = AK^a L^b$

where a and b are positive fractions.

The Cobb-Douglas production function is often used in its following form:

$$Q = AK^a L^{(1-a)}$$

Four important properties of the Cobb-Douglas production function was discussed in detail in the unit. One of which is that the powers *a* and *b* in the above production function (the first equation) represent the elasticity coefficient of output for K and L respectively.

6.0 Tutor-Marked Assignment

Given the Cobb-Douglas production function: $Q = 100K^{0.4}L^{0.6}$, derive mathematically the output elasticities of capital (K) and labour (L), respectively.

7.0 References

1. Dwivedi, D. N. (2002) *Managerial Economics, sixth edition* (New Delhi: Vikas Publishing House Ltd).

2. Haessuler, E. F. and Paul, R. S. (1976), *Introductory Mathematical Analysis for Students of Business and Economics, 2nd edition* (Reston Virginia: Reston Publishing Company)

UNIT 14: DEGREES OF PRODUCTION FUNCTIONS, ECONOMIES OF SCALE, RETURNS, AND OPTIMAL INPUT COMBINATIONS

Content
1.0 Introduction
2.0 Objectives
3.0 Degrees of production Function, Economies of scale, Returns to scale, and Optimal Input Combinations
3.1 Degree of Production Functions and Returns to Scale
3.2 Economies and Diseconomies of Scale
3.3 Optimal Input Combinations
3.4 Self-Assessment Exercise
4.0 Conclusion
5.0 Summary
6.0 Tutor-Marked Assignment
7.0 References

1.0 Introduction
This unit discusses four important production concepts that a manager must know in order to be in the hem of affairs in any production decision. As the unit title indicates, these concepts include: (i) degrees of production functions; (ii) economies of scale in production; (iii) returns to scale; and, (iv) optimal input combinations.

2.0 Objectives
Having gone through this unit, you should be able to:
1. Be more informed on the issues involving production decisions than ever.
2. Make efficient and effective.
3. Understand the managerial implications of economies and diseconomies of scale in production.

3.0 Degrees of production Function, Economies of scale, Returns to scale, and Optimal Input Combinations

3.1 Degree of Production Functions and Returns to Scale
The famous laws of returns to scale can be explained through production functions. Assume generally a production function involving two variables capital (K) and labour (L), and one commodity, X. The production function may be expressed in the form:

$$Q_x = f(K, L) \qquad (3.1.1)$$

Q_x denotes the quantity produced of commodity X. Assume also that the production function is *homogeneous*, that is, when all inputs are increased in the same proportion, the proportion can be factored out mathematically. If when all inputs are increased by a certain proportion (say, k) and output increases by the same proportion (k), the production function is said to be homogeneous of degree 1. A production function of homogeneous of degree 1 is expressed as follows:

$$kQ_x = f(kK, kL) \qquad (3.1.2)$$
$$= k(K, L)$$

A homogeneous production function of degree 1 implies ***constant returns to scale***. Equation (3.1.2) indicates that increases in the inputs K and L by a multiple of k, will increase output, Q_x, by the same multiple, k, implying constant returns to scale.

Note that increasing inputs, say K and L in the same proportion may result in increasing or diminishing returns to scale. Simply stated, it is likely that increases in all the inputs in certain proportion may not result in increase in output in the same proportion. If all the inputs are doubled, for example, output may not be doubled, it may increase by les than or more than double. In this case, the production function can be expressed as:

$$hQ_x = f(kK, kL) \tag{3.1.3}$$

where h denotes h-times increase in output, Q_x, as a result of k-times increase in inputs, K and L. The proportion, h may be greater than k, equal to k, or less than k. This touches on ***the three laws of returns to scale***:
(i) If h = k, production function reveals constant returns to scale
(ii) If h > k, production function reveals increasing returns to scale
(iii) If h < k, the production function reveals decreasing returns to scale.

Observe that in the production function, equation (3.1.2), k has an exponent equal to 1 (that is, $k = k^1$), hence, it is of homogeneous of degree 1. In general, the exponent of k can take the letter r, where $r \neq 1$. A production function is therefore, said to be homogeneous of degree r when if all the inputs are multiplied by k, output increases by a multiple of K^r. That is, if,
$$f(kK, kL) = K^r(K, L) = k^rQ \tag{3.1.4},$$
then the production function (equation, 3.1.4) is homogeneous of degree r.

From this production function, the laws of returns to scale can again be derived as follows:
(i) If k > 1, and r < 1, production function reveals decreasing returns to scale
(ii) If k > 1, and r > 1, production function reveals increasing returns to scale
(iii) If k > 1, and r = 1, production function reveals constant returns to scale.

Consider the following multiplicative form of a production function:
$$Q = K^{0.25}L^{0.50} \tag{3.1.5}$$
If K and L are multiplied by k, and output increases by a multiple of h, then
$hQ = (kK)^{0.25}(kL)^{0.50}$.

factoring out k, you get:

$$hQ = k^{0.25 + 0.50}[K^{0.25}L^{0.50}]$$
$$= k^{0.75}[K^{0.25}L^{0.50}] \tag{3.1.6}$$

According to equation (4.14), $h = k^{0.75}$ and r = 0.75, implying that r < 1, and, h < k. It follows that the production function (equation, 3.1.5) shows decreasing returns to scale.

Consider another production function of the form:

$$Q = f(K, L, X) = K^{0.75} L^{1.25} X^{0.50} \qquad (3.1.7)$$

Multiplying K, L, and X by k, Q increases by a multiple of h:

$$hQ = (kK)^{0.75} (kL)^{1.25} (kX)^{0.50}$$

Again factoring out k, you get:

$$hQ = k^{(0.75+1.25+0.50)}[K^{0.75} L^{1.25} X^{0.50}]$$
$$= k^{2.5}[K^{0.75} L^{1.25} X^{0.50}]$$

Observe that in this case, $h = k2.5$ and $r = 2.5$, so that $h > k$. Thus, production function (equation, 3.1.7) depicts increasing returns to scale.

3.2 Economies and Diseconomies of Scale

It can be shown that Long-run average cost decreases with the expansion of production scale up to a certain optimum level, and then begins to rise. This behaviour of the long-run average cost is cost by the economies and diseconomies of scale. Economies of scale gives rise to cost savings, while diseconomies of scale leads to cost increases. Economies and diseconomies of scale determine also the *returns to scale* in production. Increasing returns to scale operates until economies of scale are greater than the economies of scale. When economies of scale and diseconomies of scale are in balance, returns to scale are constant. In the discussions that follow, we examine the various kinds of economies and diseconomies of scale.

3.2.1 Economies of Scale.

Economies of scale are of two different categories:
(i) Internal or Real economies; and,
(ii) External or Pecuniary Economies.

i. *Internal Economies*. Internal or 'real economies' arise from the expansion of the plant size of the firm and are internalized. This implies that internal economies are exclusively available to the expanding firm. Internal economies are often classified under the categories:
(a) Economies in production;
(b) Economies in marketing;
(c) Managerial economies; and,
(d) Economies in transport and storage.

Economies in Production. Economies in production arise from two basic sources: (a) technological advantages; and, (b) advantages of division of labour and specialization.

Economies in Marketing. Economies in marketing arise from large-scale purchase of raw materials and other material inputs, as well as large-scale selling of the firm's own products. Economies in marketing the firm's own product are associated with: (a) economies in advertisement cost;

(i) economies in large-scale distribution through wholesalers; and (c) large-scale economies.

Managerial Economies. These arise from (a) specialization in management; and, (b) mechanization of managerial functions.

Economies in Transport and Storage costs arise from full utilization of transport and storage facilities.

ii. **External or Pecuniary Economies of Scale.** These kind of economies of scale accrue to the expanding firms from the advantages arising outside the firm, from the input market, for example. Pecuniary economies accrue to the large-size firms in the form of discounts and concessions on: (i) large-scale purchase of raw materials; (ii) large-scale acquisition of external finance; (iii) massive advertisement campaigns; (iv) large-scale hiring of means of transport and warehouse, and the like.

3.2.2 Diseconomies of Scale

Diseconomies of scale represent disadvantages that arise due to the expansion of scale of production, leading to a rise in production cost. This may be *internal* or *external*.

i. **Internal Diseconomies of Scale.** Economies of scale has some limit, which is reached when the advantages of division of labour and managerial staff have been fully exploited; excess plant capacity; excess warehouse capacity; excess transport and communication capacity, and the like.

(ii) External Diseconomies of Scale. These are the disadvantages that originate outside the firm: in the input markets, and due to natural constraints, especially in agriculture and extractive industries. With the expansion of the industry, for example, the discounts and concessions that are available on bulk purchases of inputs, as well as concessions on finance will eventually come to an end. Increasing demand for inputs also put pressure on the input markets leading to increase in input prices that will further lead to rises in production costs.

3.3 Optimal Input Combinations

Economists are of the opinion that profit-maximising firms seek to minimise costs for a given level of output, or to maximise its output for a given total cost. The two major instruments in the maximisation of output are the ***Isoquants curves*** and ***Isocost line***, often referred to as the ***budget constraint line.*** The logic of isoquant tells you that a given level of output can be produced with different input combinations. Given the input prices, however, only one of the input combinations would be the least cost combination. The least-cost combination represents the input combination for which the budget constraint line is tangent to the isoquant curve. This is the point for which the slope of the budget constraint line equals the slope of the isoquant curve, as indicated by figure 3.3.1 below.

Figure 3.3.1: Least-Cost Combination of Inputs

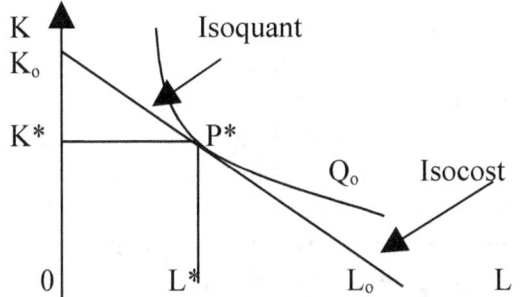

According to figure 4.1, the least-cost combination of the inputs, capital (K) and labour (L) is at the point (P*) for which the isocost line, K_oL_o is tangent to the isoquant curve, Q_o. At this point, the optimal combination of capital (K) and labour (L) is OK* of K and OL* of L. This combination is optimal since it satisfies the least-cost criterion:

$$\frac{MP_L}{MP_K} = \frac{P_L}{P_K} \qquad (3.3.1)$$

Or $$\frac{MP_L}{P_L} = \frac{MP_K}{P_K} \qquad (3.3.2)$$

where MP_L and MP_K are marginal products of labour and capital, respectively, and P_L and P_K are prices of labour and capital, respectively.

The above least-cost criterion can be translated in values terms by multiplying the marginal productivities of capital (MP_K) and labour (MP_L) each by the product price (P) to obtain the marginal revenue product of labour (MRP_L) and the marginal revenue product of capital (MRP_K), and taking ratios to get:

$$\frac{MP_L.P}{MP_K.P} = \frac{MRP_L}{MRP_K} \qquad (3.3.3)$$

Equation (3.3.3) can be related to the ratio of input prices as follows:

$$\frac{P_L}{P_K} = \frac{MRP_L}{MRP_K}$$

Or, $$\frac{MRP_L}{P_L} = \frac{MRP_K}{P_K} \qquad (3.3.4)$$

It can be inferred from equation (3.3.4) that least-cost or optimum input combination requires that the marginal revenue productivity ratio of factors should be equal to their price ratios, or that the marginal revenue productivity and factor price ratios of all the inputs must be equal.

3.3.1 Effect of Changes in Input Prices on the Optimal Combination of Inputs

Changes in input prices affect the optimal combination of inputs at different magnitudes, depending on the nature of input price change. If all input prices change in the same proportion, the relative prices of inputs (that is the slope of the budget constraint or isocost line) remain unaffected. But when input prices change at different rates in the same direction, or change at different rates in the opposite direction, or price of only one input changes while the prices of other inputs remain constant, the relative prices of the inputs will change. This change in relative input-prices changes both the input-combinations and the level of output. The change in input-combinations is as a result of the substitution effect of change in relative prices of inputs. A change in relative prices of inputs would imply that some inputs have become cheaper in relation to others. Cost-minimising firms attempt to substitute relatively cheaper inputs for the more expense ones. This refers to the ***substitution effect*** of relative input-price changes.

The effect of change in input prices on optimal input combinations is illustrated by figure 3.3.2 below.

Figure 3.3.2: Substitution Effect of Changes in Input Prices

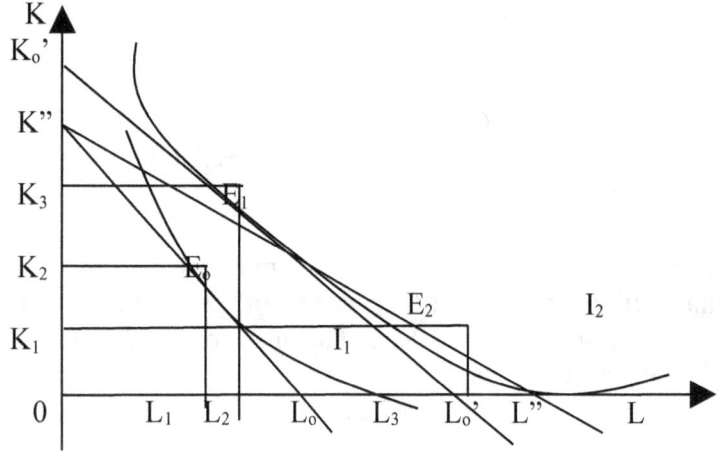

We assume that, given the price of capital (P_k) and price of labour (P_L), and the total resources as indicated by the isocost line, $K"L_o$, the representative firm's optimum input-combination is given by point E_o in figure 3.3.2. Suppose that P_L decreases (P_k remaining constant), resulting in a new isocost, $K"L"$, which is tangent to the isoquant, I_2 at point E_2. At this point, the firm's new optimum combination of inputs becomes $OK_1 + OL_3$. It follows that the decrease in price of labour (P_L) has given rise to the reduction of capital input by the amount K_1K_2 and increment of labour input by L_1L_3. The change in the input combination is referred to as the ***price effect*** of the decrease in the price of labour. This price effect is composed of substitution and budget effects, where the substitution effect is represented by the difference between price effect and budget effect. Thus,

Substitution effect = Price effect – Budget effect.

From figure 2, the Price effect = L_1L_3, and,

Budget effect = L_1L_2
Substitution effect = $L_1L_3 - L_1L_2 = L_2L_3$

We conclude therefore, that a firm's input combination changes with a change in the price of a given input, all things being equal. In this illustration, the firm employs more of the cheaper input (L) and less of the more expensive one (K). The level of output also changes, as you can infer from figure 3.3.2.

3.4 Self-Assessment Exercise

With the appropriate diagram, discuss the effect of a decrease in the price of labour input on the optimal input combination, assuming a production function involving capital (K) and labour (L).

4.0 Conclusion

Some of the important production concepts learned from this unit involve: degrees of production function; economies and diseconomies of scale; returns to scale; and, optimal input combinations. We learned that Economies of scale are of two different categories:
(i) Internal or Real economies; and,
(ii) External or Pecuniary Economies.
Diseconomies of scale represent disadvantages that arise due to the expansion of scale of production, leading to a rise in production cost. This may be *internal* or *external*.

5.0 Summary

A production function is said to be ***homogeneous of degree 1*** if when all inputs are increased by a certain proportion, output is increased by the same proportion. For instance, if when all inputs are increased by a certain proportion (say, k) and output increases by the same proportion (k), the production function is said to be homogeneous of degree 1. A homogeneous production function of degree 1 implies ***constant returns to scale***. In general, given the production function:
$hQ_x = f(kK, kL)$
where h denotes h-times increase in output, Q_x, as a result of k-times increase in inputs, K and L. The proportion, h may be greater than k, equal to k, or less than k. This touches on ***the three laws of returns to scale***:
(i) If h = k, production function reveals constant returns to scale
(ii) If h > k, production function reveals increasing returns to scale
(iii) If h < k, the production function reveals decreasing returns to scale.

Economies of scale gives rise to cost savings, while diseconomies of scale leads to cost increases. Economies and diseconomies of scale determine also the *returns to scale* in production. Increasing returns to scale operates until economies of scale are greater than the economies of scale. When economies of scale and diseconomies of scale are in balance, returns to scale are constant.

The least-cost combination of inputs is also the optimal input combinations. This is the combination of inputs for which the marginal revenue products of the inputs are equal.

6.0 Tutor-Marked Assignment

Determine whether the following production functions show constant, increasing, or decreasing returns to scale:
(a) $Q = L^{0.60} K^{0.40}$
(b) $Q = 5K^{0.5} L^{0.3}$
(c) $Q = 4L + 2K$

7.0 References

Dwivedi, D. N. (2002) *Managerial Economics, sixth edition* (New Delhi: Vikas Publishing House Ltd).

UNIT 15: THE THEORY OF COST

Content
1.0 Introduction
2.0 Objectives
3.0 The Theory of Production Costs

3.1 The Business Cost Concepts
3.2 Self-Assessment Exercise
4.0 Conclusion
5.0 Summary
6.0 Tutor-Marked Assignment
7.0 References

1.0 Introduction
Business decisions are generally taken based on the monetary values of inputs and outputs. Note that the quantity of inputs multiplied by their respective unit prices will give the monetary value or the *cost of production.* Production cost is an important factor in all business decisions, especially those decisions concerning:
    (a) the location of the weak points in production management;
    (b) cost minimisation
    (c) finding the optimal level of output;
    (d) determination of price and dealers' margin; and,
    (e) estimation of the costs of business operation.

In this unit, we present briefly the cost concepts applicable to business decisions.

2.0 Objectives
At the end of this unit, you will be expected to:
1. Be familiar with the theory of production costs
2. Estimate the costs of business operation
3. Minimise production costs
4. Make plausible costing decisions.

3.0 The Theory of Production Costs

3.1 The Business Cost Concepts
The cost concepts are theoretically grouped under two over-lapping categories:
(i) Concepts used for accounting purposes; and,
(ii) Analytical cost concepts used in economic analysis of business activities.

3.1.1 Accounting Cost Concepts
The accounting cost concepts include:
1. Opportunity Cost and Actual or Explicit Cost. Opportunity cost can be seen as the expected returns from the second best use of an economic resource which is foregone due to the scarcity of the resources. Some scholars refer to opportunity cost as *alternative cost.* There would be no opportunity cost if the resources available to the society were unlimited.

Associated with the concept of opportunity cost is the concept of *economic rent* or *economic profit.* Economic rent is the excess of earning from investment over and above the expected profit. The business implication of this concept is that investing in a given project will be preferred so long as its economic rent is greater than zero or positive.

Additionally, if firms know the economic rent of various alternative uses of their resources, it will aid them in the choice of the best investment avenue.

The actual or explicit costs are those out-of-pocket costs of labour, materials, machine, plant building and other factors of production.

2. *Business and Full Costs*. All the expenses incurred to carry out a business are referred to as business costs. These are similar to actual or real costs, and include all the payments and contractual obligations made by the firm, together with the book cost of depreciation on plant and equipment. Business costs are those used in calculating business profits and losses and for filing returns for income tax and for other legal purposes.

Full costs include business costs, opportunity costs and normal profit, while normal profit represents a necessary minimum earning in addition to the opportunity cost, which a firm must receive to remain in business.

3. *Explicit and Implicit/Imputed Costs.* These are costs falling under business costs and are those entered in the books of accounts. Payments for wages and salaries, materials, insurance premium, depreciation charges are examples of *explicit costs*. These costs involve cash payments and are recorded in accounting practices.

Those costs that do not involve cash outlays or payments and do not appear in the business accounting system are referred to as *implicit* or *imputed* costs. Implicit costs are not taken into account while calculating the loss or gains of the business, though they form an important consideration in whether or not a factor will be continued in use for the day to day operations of the business. The explicit and implicit costs together (explicit + implicit costs) form the ***economic cost.***

4. *Out-of-Pocket and Book Costs.* Expenditure items that involve cash payments or cash transfers, both recurring and non-recurring, are referred to in economics as *out-of-pocket costs*. All the explicit costs including wages, rent, interest, cost of materials, maintenance, transport expenditures, and the like are in this classification. On the contrary, there exists some actual business costs which do not involve cash payments, but a provision is made in the books of account and they are taken into account while finalizing the profit and loss accounts. Such costs are known as *book costs*. These are somehow, payments made by a firm to itself.

3.1.2 Analytical Cost Concepts Used in Economic Analysis of Business Activities.

The analytical cost concepts include:
6. Fixed and Variable Costs
7. Total, Average, and Marginal Costs
8. Short-Run and Long-Run Costs
9. Incremental Costs and Sunk Costs

10. Historical and Replacement Costs
11. Private and Social Costs

1. Fixed and Variable Costs. *Fixed costs* are those costs that are fixed in volume for a certain level of output. They do not vary with output. They remain constant regardless of the level of output. Fixed costs include:
(i) Cost of managerial and administrative staff; (ii) Depreciation of machinery; (iii) Land maintenance, and the like. Fixed costs are normally short-term concepts because, in the long-run, all costs must vary.

Variable Costs are those that vary with variations in output. These include: (i) Cost of raw materials; (ii) Running costs of fixed capital, such as fuel, repairs, routine maintenance expenditure, direct labour charges associated with output levels; and (iii) the Costs of all other inputs that may vary with the level of output.

2. Total, Average, and Marginal Costs. The *Total Cost (TC)* refers to the total expenditure on the production of goods and services. It includes both explicit and implicit costs. The explicit costs themselves are made up of fixed and variable costs. For a given level of output, the total cost is determined by the cost function.

The *Average cost (AC)* is obtained by dividing total cost (TC) by total output (Q). Thus,
$$AC = \frac{TC}{Q} \quad (3.1.1)$$

Marginal Cost (MC) is the addition to total cost on account of producing one additional unit of a product. It is the cost of the marginal unit produced. Marginal cost of output can be computed as $TC_n - TC_{n-1}$, where n represents the current number of units produced, and n-1 represents the previous number of units produced. MC can also be computed by the following relationship:
$$MC = \frac{\text{Change in TC}}{\text{Change in Q}} = \frac{\Delta TC}{\Delta Q} \quad (3.1.2)$$
If the total cost (TC) is in a functional form, MC can be computed by the derivative:
$$MC = \frac{dTC}{dQ} \quad (3.1.3)$$

3. Short-Run and Long-Run Costs. *Short-Run Costs* are costs which change as desired output changes, size of the firm remaining constant. These costs are often referred to as variable costs. *Long-Run costs,* on the other hand are costs incurred on the firm's fixed assets, such as plant, machinery, building, and the like.

In the long-run, all costs become variable costs as the size of the firm or scale of production increases. Put differently, long-run costs are associated with changes in the size and type of plant.

4. Incremental Costs and Sunk Costs. Conceptually, *incremental costs* are closely related to the concept of marginal cost, but with a relatively wider connotation. While marginal cost refers to the cost of extra or one more unit of output, incremental cost refers to the total additional cost associated with the decision to expand output or to add a new variety of product. The concept of incremental cost is based on the fact that, in the real world, it is not practicable to employ factors for each unit of output separately due to lack of perfect divisibility of inputs. Incremental costs also arise as a result of change in product line, addition or introduction of a new product, replacement of worn out plant and machinery, replacement of old technique of production with a new one, and the like.

The *Sunk costs* are those costs that cannot be altered, increased or decreased, by varying the rate of output. For instance, once management decides to make incremental investment expenditure and the funds are allocated and spent, all preceding costs are considered to be the sunk costs since they accord to the prior commitment and cannot be reversed or recovered when there is a change in market conditions or a change in business decisions.

5. Historical and Replacement Costs. *Historical cost* refers to the cost an asset acquired in the past, whereas, *replacement cost* refers to the outlay made for replacing an old asset. These concepts derive from the unstable nature of price behaviour. When prices become stable over time, other things being equal, historical and replacement costs will be at par with each other.

6. Private and Social Costs. Private and social costs are those costs which arise as a result of the functioning of a firm, but neither are normally reflected in the business decisions nor are explicitly borne by the firm. Costs in this category are borne by the society. It follows that the total cost generated in the course of doing business may be divided into two categories:
(i) those paid out by the firm; and, (ii) those not paid or borne by the firm, including the use of resources that are freely available plus the disutility created in the process of production. Costs under the first category are known as *private costs*. Those of the second category are known as *external* or social costs. Examples of such social costs include: water pollution from oil refineries, air pollution costs by mills and factories located near a city, and the like. From a firm's point of view, such costs are classified as *external costs*, and from the society's point of view, they are classified as *social costs*.

The relevance of the concept of social costs is more pronounced in the cost-benefit analysis of the overall impact of a firm's operation in the society as a whole, and in working out the social cost of private gains.

3.2 Self-Assessment Exercise
How do incremental and sunk costs differ from marginal costs.

4.0 Conclusion
This unit focused on the general cost concepts. The cost concepts are theoretically grouped under two over-lapping categories:
(i) Concepts used for accounting purposes; and,

(ii) Analytical cost concepts used in economic analysis of business activities.

The accounting cost concepts include:
(i) Opportunity costs and explicit costs
(ii) Business and full costs
(iii) Explicit and imputed costs
(iv) Out-of-pocket and Book costs

The analytical cost concepts include:
    12. Fixed and Variable Costs
    13. Total, Average, and Marginal Costs
    14. Short-Run and Long-Run Costs
    15. Incremental Costs and Sunk Costs
    16. Historical and Replacement Costs
    17. Private and Social Costs

5.0 Summary
The unit's discussions can be summarised as follows:

First, opportunity cost can be seen as the expected returns from the second best use of an economic resource which is foregone due to the scarcity of the resources. Some scholars refer to opportunity cost as *alternative cost*. There would be no opportunity cost if the resources available to the society were unlimited.

Associated with the concept of opportunity cost is the concept of ***economic rent*** or ***economic profit.*** Economic rent is the excess of earning from investment over and above the expected profit. The business implication of this concept is that investing in a given project will be preferred so long as its economic rent is greater than zero or positive.

Second, all the expenses incurred to carry out a business are referred to as business costs.

Third, those costs that do not involve cash outlays or payments and do not appear in the business accounting system are referred to as *implicit* or *imputed* costs.

Fourth, The analytical cost concepts used in economic analysis of business activities include: (i) Fixed and Variable Costs. *Fixed costs* are those costs that are fixed in volume for a certain level of output. *Variable Costs* are those that vary with variations in output. (ii) Total, Average, and Marginal Costs. (iii) Short-Run and Long-Run Costs. *Short-Run Costs* are costs which change as desired output changes, size of the firm remaining constant. These costs are often referred to as variable costs. *Long-Run costs,* on the other hand are costs incurred on the firm's fixed assets, such as plant, machinery, building, and the like. (iv) Incremental Costs and Sunk Costs. *Incremental costs* are closely related to the concept of marginal cost, but with a relatively wider connotation. While *marginal cost* refers to the cost of extra or one more unit of output, incremental cost refers to the total additional cost associated with the decision to expand output or to add a new variety of product. The *Sunk costs* are those costs that cannot be altered, increased or decreased, by varying the rate of output. (v) Historical and Replacement Costs. *Historical cost* refers to the cost an asset acquired in the past, whereas, *replacement cost* refers to the outlay made for replacing an old asset. (vi) Private and Social Costs. Private and social costs are those costs which arise as a result of the functioning of a firm, but neither are normally reflected in the business decisions nor are explicitly borne by the firm. Costs in this category are borne by the society.

6.0 Tutor-Marked Assignment
Briefly present what you think are the major differences between accounting costs and economic costs.

7.0 References
Dwivedi, D. N. (2002) ***Managerial Economics, sixth edition*** (New Delhi: Vikas Publishing House Ltd).

UNIT 16: THE THEORY OF COST: COST-OUTPUT RELATIONS

Content
1.0 Introduction
2.0 Objectives
3.0 Cost-Output Relations
3.1 The Cost Functions

3.2 Cost Minimisation
3.3 Output Optimisation in the Short-Run
3.4 Self-Assessment Exercise
4.0 Conclusion
5.0 Summary
6.0 Tutor-Marked Assignment
7.0 References

1.0 Introduction
The theory of costs basically deal with costs in relation to output changes. In other words, they deal with cost-output relations. The basic economic principle states that *total cost increases with increase in output.* However, what is important from a theoretical and marginal point of view is not the absolute increase in total cost, but the direction of change in the average cost (AC) and the marginal cost (MC). The direction of changes in AC and MC will depend on the nature of the cost function. In this unit, we examine in detail the cost-output relations.

2.0 Objectives
Having gone through this unit, you will be expected to:
1. Expand your knowledge of the theory of costs
2. Know the theoretical cost-output relations
3. Apply cost functions in the minimisation of costs of production.

3.0 Cost-Output Relations
A cost function is a symbolic statement of the technological relationship between the cost and output. Generally, cost functions take the following form:

$C = TC = f(Q)$, and $\Delta Q > 0$,

where Q represents output level.

In addition, the specific form of the cost function depends on the time framework for cost analysis: short-or long-run. Thus, there exists short-run cost function and long-run cost function. Accordingly, cost-output relationship are analysed in short run and long-run frameworks.

3.1 The Cost Functions

3.1.1 The Short-Run Cost Function.
Cost-output relations are normally determined by the cost function and are exhibited by cost curves. The shape of cost curves depends on the nature of the cost function which are derived from actual cost data. Cost functions may take a variety of forms, yielding

different kinds of cost curves, including *linear, quadratic, and cubic cost* curves arising from the corresponding functions. The functions are as illustrated below:

1. Linear Cost Function. A linear cost function is of the form:
$$TC = C = a + bQ \qquad (3.1.1)$$
where a = Total Fix Cost (TFC)
bQ = Total Variable Cost (TVC)

The Average and Marginal cost functions can be obtained from the Total Cost Function (equation 3.1.1) as follows:

$$\text{Average Cost (AC)} = \frac{TC}{Q} = \frac{a+bQ}{Q} = a/Q + b$$

$$\text{Marginal Cost (MC)} = \frac{dTC}{dQ} = b$$

2. Quadratic Cost Function. The quadratic cost function is of the form:

$$TC = C = a + bQ + Q^2 \qquad (3.1.2)$$

From the quadratic cost function (equation 3.1.2), we can obtain the Average and Marginal cost functions as follows:

$$AC = \frac{TC}{Q} = \frac{a+bQ+Q^2}{Q} = a/Q + b + Q$$

$$MC = \frac{dTC}{dQ} = b + 2Q$$

Example, if $TC = C = 150 + 10Q + Q^2$
Then,

$$AC = \frac{150 + 10Q + Q^2}{Q}$$
$$= 150/Q + 10 + Q$$

$$MC = \frac{dTC}{dQ} = 10 + 2Q$$

3. Cubic Cost Function. The cubic cost function is of the form:

$$TC = C = a + bQ - cQ^2 + dQ^3 \qquad (3.1.3)$$

The corresponding Average Cost (AC) and Marginal Cost (MC) functions can be derived as:

$$AC = \frac{TC}{Q} = \frac{a + bQ - cQ^2 + dQ^3}{Q}$$

$$= a/Q + b - cQ + dQ^2$$

$$MC = \frac{dTC}{dQ} = b - 2cQ + 3dQ^2$$

Assume that the cost function is empirically and explicitly estimated as:

$$TC = 10 + 6Q - 0.9Q^2 + 0.05Q^3 \qquad (3.1.4)$$

And,

$$TVC = 6Q - 0.9Q^2 + 0.05Q^3 \qquad (3.1.5)$$

Based on equations 3.1.4 and 3.1.5, the TC and TVC, respectively is calculated for Q = 1 to 10 and presented in table 3.1.1, and graphically illustrated in figure 3.1.1.

Table 3.1.1: Cost-Output Relations

Q	FC	TVC	TC	AFC	AVC	AC	MC
(1)	(2)	(3)	(4)	(5)	(6)	(7)	(8)
0	10	0.0	10.00	-	-	-	-
1	10	5.15	15.15	10.00	5.15	15.15	5.15
2	10	8.80	18.80	5.00	4.40	9.40	3.65
3	10	11.25	21.25	3.33	3.75	7.08	2.45
4	10	12.80	22.80	2.50	3.20	5.70	1.55
5	10	13.75	23.75	2.00	2.75	4.75	0.95
6	10	14.40	24.40	1.67	2.40	4.07	0.65
7	10	15.05	25.05	1.43	2.15	3.58	0.65
8	10	16.00	26.00	1.25	2.00	3.25	0.95
9	10	17.55	27.55	1.11	1.95	3.06	1.55
10	10	20.00	30.00	1.00	2.00	3.00	2.45

Using equations (3.1.4) and (3.1.5), you can derive the behavioural equations for the average fixed cost (AFC), average variable cost (AVC), average total cost (ATC), and marginal cost (MC) as follows:

$$AFC = FC/Q = 10/Q$$

$$AVC = TVC/Q = \frac{6Q - 0.9Q^2 + 0.05Q^3}{Q} = 6 - 0.9Q + 0.05Q^2$$

$$ATC = TC/Q = \frac{10 + 6Q - 0.9Q^2 + 0.05Q^3}{Q}$$

$$= 10/Q + 6 - 0.9Q + 0.05Q^2$$

$$MC = \frac{dTC}{dQ} = 6 - 1.8Q + 0.15Q^2$$

3.2 Cost Minimisation

In its simplest form, the critical value of output (Q) in respect of the average variable cost (AVC) is the value that minimises average variable cost. The average variable cost will be at its minimum when its rate of change $\{\frac{d(AVC)}{dQ}\} = 0$. This can be accomplished by differentiating the AVC function with respect to output (Q). Thus, form our examples,

$$AVC = 6 - 0.9Q + 0.05Q^2$$

$$\frac{d(AVC)}{dQ} = -0.9 + 0.10Q$$

Setting this equal zero, you get:

$-0.9 + 0.10Q = 0$

$0.10Q = 0.9$

$Q = 9$

It follows that critical value of output (Q) in respect of the average variable cost is 9 units. From table 3.1.1, we observe that at the output level Q = 9, the minimum average variable cost is N1.95.

The same argument can be made for average total cost (ATC). Given the ATC function, you can set the derivative with respect to Q $\{(\frac{d(ATC)}{dQ}\} = 0$, and solve for Q to obtain the level of output that minimises average total cost.

3.3 Output Optimisation in the Short-Run

The optimum level of output in the short-run is the level of output for which the average cost (AC) of production equals the marginal cost (MC). That is, for optimum output, AC = MC in the short-run.

Suppose the short-run cost function is given by:

$$C = 200 + 5Q + 2Q^2 \qquad (3.3.1)$$

$$AC = \frac{200 + 5Q + 2Q^2}{Q}$$

$$= 200/Q + 5 + 2Q \qquad (3.3.2)$$

$$MC = \frac{dC}{dQ} = 5 + 4Q \qquad (3.3.3)$$

By using AC = MC at optimum, and solving for Q, you will obtain the optimum level of output.

Thus,

$$\frac{200}{Q} + 5 + 2Q = 5 + 4Q \qquad (AC = MC)$$

$$200/Q = 2Q$$

$$2Q^2 = 200$$

$$Q^2 = 100$$

$$Q = 10$$

Thus the optimum level of output in this example is 10 units.

3.4 Self-Assessment Exercise
The shape of cost curves depends on the nature of the cost function which are derived from actual cost data. Discuss.

4.0 Conclusion
This unit has exposed you to the principles of cost-output relations. You must have learned that short-run cost functions are of different categories:
(i) the linear cost function; (ii) the quadratic cost function; and, (iii) the cubic cost function. Also, an important learning from the unit is the procedures for cost minimisation.

5.0 Summary
You may have learned from this unit that Cost-output relations are normally determined by the cost function and are exhibited by cost curves. The shape of cost curves depends on the nature of the cost function which are derived from actual cost data. Cost functions may take a variety of forms, yielding different kinds of cost curves, including *linear,*

quadratic, and cubic cost curves arising from the corresponding functions. With respect to the minimisation of production cost, you learned that In its simplest form, the critical value of output (Q) in respect of the average variable cost (AVC) is the value that minimises average variable cost. The average variable cost will be at its minimum when its rate of change $\{d(AVC)/dQ\} = 0$.

Finally, you were informed that the optimum level of output in the short-run is the level of output for which the average cost (AC) of production equals the marginal cost (MC). That is, for optimum output, AC = MC in the short-run.

6.0 Tutor-Marked Assignment

Given the cost function: $C = 1000 + 10Q^{1/2} + Q + 2Q^2$, derive the average and marginal cost functions. At 5 units of output, what are the average and marginal costs.

7.0 References
Dwivedi, D. N. (2002) ***Managerial Economics, sixth edition*** (New Delhi: Vikas Publishing House Ltd).

UNIT 17 : LONG-RUN COST-OUTPUT RELATIONS AND BREAK-EVEN ANALYSIS

Content
1.0 Introduction

2.0 Objectives
3.0 The Long-Run Cost-Output Relations and Break-Even Analysis
3.1 The Long-Run Cost-Output Relations
3.2 Break-Even Analysis: Linear Cost and Revenue Functions.
3.3 Break-Even Analysis: Non-Linear Cost and Revenue Function
3.4 Self-Assessment Exercise
4.0 Conclusion
5.0 Summary
6.0 Tutor-Marked Assignment
7.0 References

1.0 Introduction

By definition, the long-run is a period for which all inputs change or become variable. This is based on the assumption that in the long-run, supply of all inputs, including those held constant in the short-run, becomes elastic. Firms are therefore, now in a position to expand the scale of production by increasing all inputs. It follows that the long-run cost-output relations imply the relationship between the changing scale of a firm and the firm's total output, whereas in the short-run, this relationship is essentially one between the total output and the variable costs such as, labour and raw materials. In this unit, we discuss the long-run cost-output relations especially with specific reference to the firm's break-even conditions.

2.0 Objectives

At the end of this unit you will be able to:
1. Be more familiar with issues on cost-output relations
2. Make long-run cost and output decisions
3. Determine your optimum plant size

3.0 The Long-Run Cost-Output Relations and Break-Even Analysis

3.1 The Long-Run Cost-Output Relations

The *long-run cost curve (LTC)* is composed of a series of short-run cost curves. This is shown by figure 3.1.1 below:

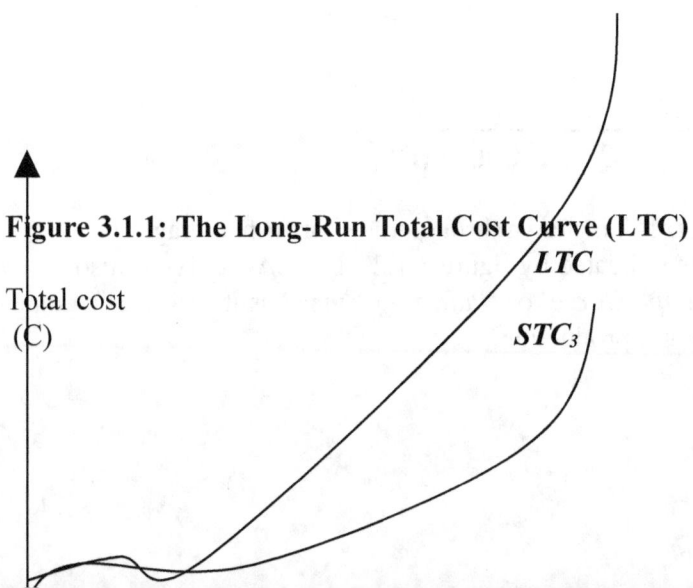

Figure 3.1.1: The Long-Run Total Cost Curve (LTC)

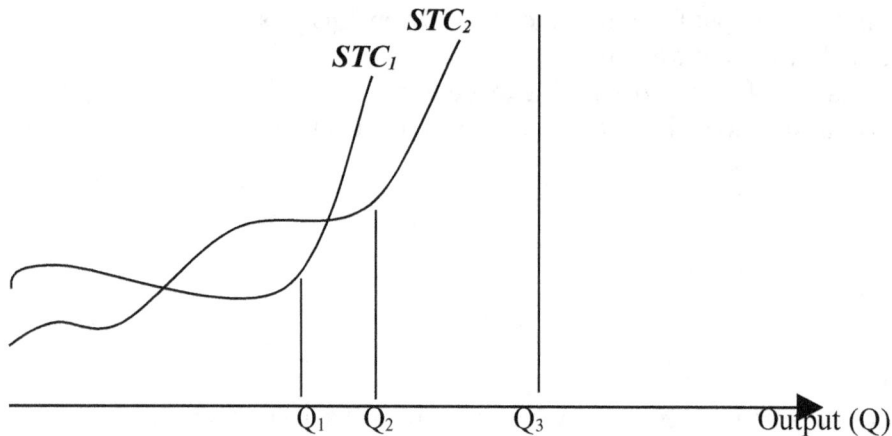

Figure 3.1.1 assumes that the firm has only one plant, with the corresponding short-run cost curve given by STC_1. Suppose the firm decides to add two more plants with associated two more short-run cost curves given by STC_2 and STC_3. The long-run total cost curve (**LTC**) is then drawn through the minimum of the short-run cost curves, STC_1, STC_2, and STC_3.

The *Long-Run Average Cost Curve (LAC)* is derived by combining the short-run average cost curves (SACs). This is as drawn in figure 3.1.2 below:

Figure 3.1.2: The Long-Run Average Cost Curve

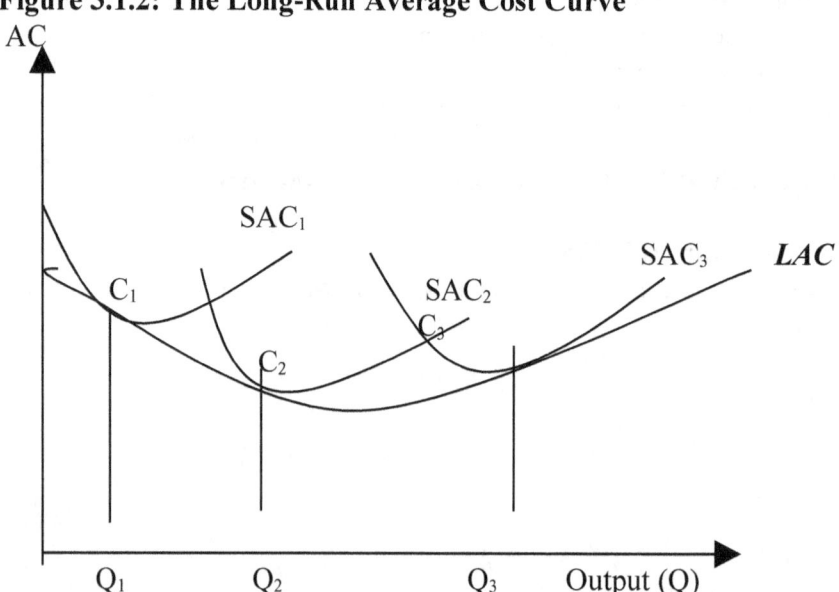

The long-run average cost curve (**LAC**) is drawn through the short-run average cost curves, SAC_1, SAC_2, and SAC_3, as indicated by figure 3.1.2. The LAC curve is also known in economics as the *'Envelope Curve'* or *'Planning Curve'* as it serves as a guide to the entrepreneur in plans to expand production.

It is obvious from the LTC in figure 3.1.1, that the long-run cost-output relations is similar to the short-run cost-output relations. With subsequent increases in output, LTC first increases at a decreasing rate, and then at an increasing rate. As a result, LAC initially decreases until the optimum utilization of the second plant capacity, and then it begins to increase. These cost-output relations follow the 'laws of returns to scale.' That is, when the scale of the firm expands, unit production cost initially decreases, but ultimately increases, as shown in figure 3.1.2. The decrease in unit cost is attributed to the internal and external economies and the eventual increase in cost, to the internal and external diseconomies.

3.1.1 Optimum Plant Size and Long-Run Cost Curves.
The short-run cost curves are extremely helpful in the determination of the *optimum utilization of a given plant*, or in the determination of the least-cost-output level. Long-run cost curves, on the other hand, can be used to show how a firm can decide on the *optimum size of the firm*.

Consequently, the optimum size of the firm is one which ensures the most efficient utilization of the resources. In practical terms, the optimum size of a firm is one in which the long-run average cost (LAC) is minimised.

3.2 Break-Even Analysis: Linear Cost and Revenue Functions.
Traditionally, the basic objective of any business firm is to maximize profit. The maximum profit does not necessarily coincide with the minimum cost, according to the traditional theory of the firm. Nevertheless, firms plan their production activities much better if the level of production for which total cost and total revenue break even is known. This implies the profitable and non-profitable range of production. The *break-even analysis*, or what is often referred to as *profit contribution analysis* is an important analytical technique used in studying the relationship between total cost, total revenue, and total profits and losses over the whole range of stipulated output. The break-even analysis is a technique of previewing profit prospects and a tool of profit planning. It integrates cost and revenue estimates to ascertain the profits and losses associated with different levels of output.

In order to exemplify the break-even analysis under linear cost and revenue conditions, you can assume a *linear cost function* and a *linear revenue function* as follows:

Cost function: $C = 100 + 10Q$ (3.2.1)

Revenue function: $R = 150Q$ (3.2.2)

The cost function (equation 3.2.1) implies a total fixed cost (TFC) of N100. Its variable cost varies at a constant rate of N10 per unit in response to increases in output. The revenue function (equation 3.2.2) implies that the market price for the firm's product is N15 per unit of sale.

Given equations 3.2.1 and 3.2.2, the break-even output can be computed algebraically in the following way:

At the break-even point,

Total Revenue (R) = Total Cost (C), so that in this example,

$15Q = 100 + 10Q$

$5Q = 100$

$Q = 20.$

It follows that the break-even level of output is 20 units. This result can be illustrated graphically in figure 3.2.1 below.

Figure 3.2.1: Break-Even Analysis: Linear Functions

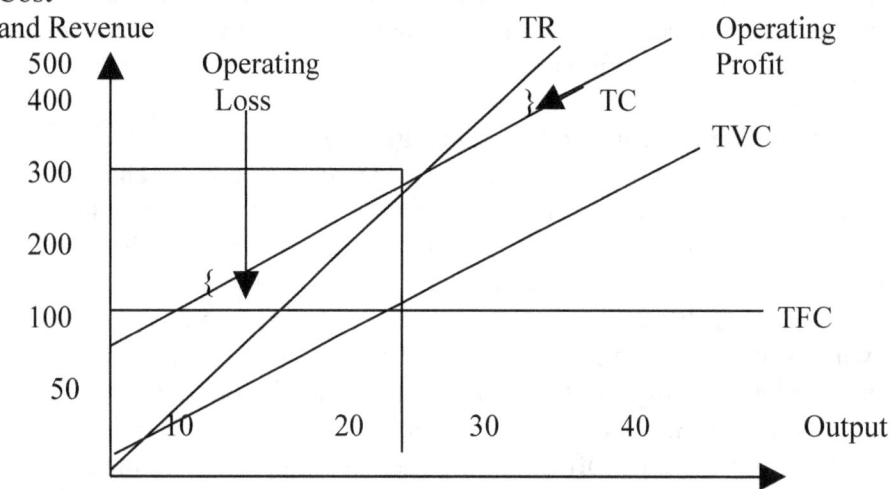

3.3 Break-Even Analysis: Non-Linear Cost and Revenue Function

The break-even analysis under non-linear cost and revenue functions is best demonstrated by the following graph. As shown in figure 3.3.1 below, the total fixed cost (TFC) line shows the fixed cost at OF, and the vertical distance between TC and TFC measures the total variable cost (TVC). The curve, TR, shows the total sales or total revenue at different output levels and at different prices. The vertical distance between the TR and TC measures the profit or loss for various levels of output.

You will observe from figure 3.3.1 that the TR and TC curves intersect each other at two points, P_1 and P_2., where TR = TC. These represent the lower and upper break-even points. For the whole range of output between OQ_1 (corresponding to the break-even point, P_1) and OQ_2 (corresponding to the break-even point, P_2), TR > TC. This implies that a firm producing more than OQ_1 and less than OQ_2 will be making profits. Put differently, the profitable range of output lies between OQ_1 and OQ_2 units of output. Producing less or more than these limits will give rise to losses.

Figure 3.3.1: Break-Even Analysis: Non-Linear Functions

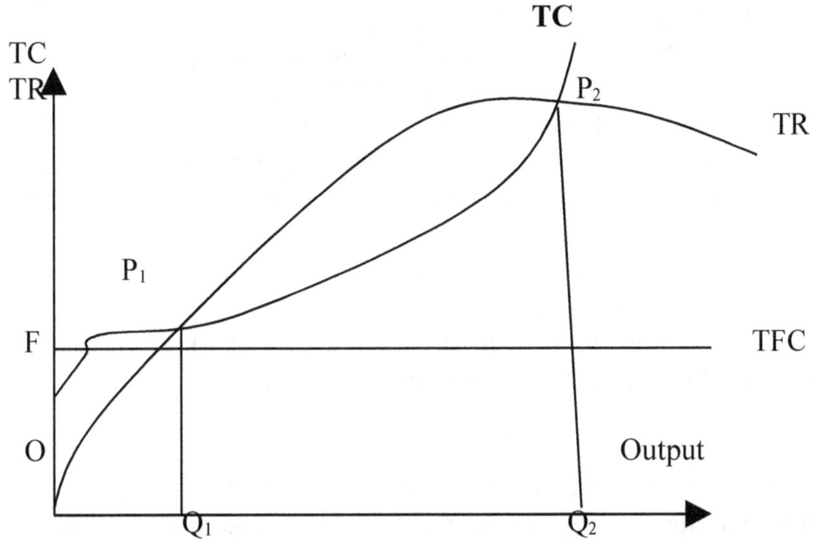

(Graph showing TC/TR on vertical axis and Output on horizontal axis, with curves TC, TR, and horizontal line TFC at level F. Points P_1 and P_2 mark break-even points at outputs Q_1 and Q_2.)

The Profit Volume (PV) Ratio.
The PV ratio is another useful tool for finding the Break-Even Point (BEP) of sales, especially for multi-purpose firms. The PV ratio is defined by the following formula:

$$PV\ Ratio = \frac{S - V}{S} \times 100$$

Where S = Selling price; and, V = average Variable cost.

For instance, if the selling price, S = N5 per unit, and average variable cost, V = N4 per unit, then:

$$PV\ Ratio = \frac{5 - 4}{5} \times 100$$
$$= 20\ percent$$

The Break-even point (BEP) in sales value is calculated by dividing the fixed expenses (F) by the PV ratio. Thus,

$$BEP\ (Sales\ value) = \frac{Fixed\ Expenses}{PV\ Ratio} = \frac{F}{\frac{S-V}{S}}$$

3.4 Self-Assessment Exercise
Describe briefly how a firm can decide on its optimum plant size using the long-run cost curve.

4.0 Conclusion

You may have learned from this unit that the long-run in any business life is very important and must be taken as such. The long-run has been defined as a period for which all inputs change or become variable. This is based on the assumption that in the long-run, supply of all inputs, including those held constant in the short-run, becomes elastic. In addition, the short-run cost curves are extremely helpful in the determination of the *optimum utilization of a given plant*, or in the determination of the least-cost-output level. Long-run cost curves, on the other hand, can be used to show how a firm can decide on the *optimum size of the firm*. Finally, the unit informs you that the *break-even analysis*, or what is often referred to as *profit contribution analysis* is an important analytical technique used in studying the relationship between total cost, total revenue, and total profits and losses over the whole range of stipulated output.

5.0 Summary

Our discussion in the unit can be summarised in the following statements:

1. Business managers must plan for the long-run administration of costs revenues and profits. This is so because in the long run, firms will be in a position to expand the scale of production by increasing all inputs.
2. In the long-run, with increases in output, the total cost of production first increases at a decreasing rate, and then at an increasing rate. As a result, the long-run average cost initially decreases until the optimum utilization of the new plant capacity, and then it begins to increase. These cost-output relations follow the 'laws of returns to scale.'
3. Firms are assumed to plan their production activities much better if the level of production for which total cost and total revenue break even is known. This implies the profitable and non-profitable range of production. The break-even analysis, or what is often referred to as profit contribution analysis is an important analytical technique used in studying the relationship between total cost, total revenue, and total profits and losses over the whole range of stipulated output. The break-even analysis is a technique of previewing profit prospects and a tool of profit planning.

6.0 Tutor-Marked Assignment

The profit and loss data of an enterprise for a given period are as follows:

Naira (N)

Net Sales	100,000
Cost of goods sold:	
Variable Cost	40,000
Fixed Cost	10,000
Gross Profit	50,000
Selling Costs:	
Variable Cost	10,000
Fixed Cost	5,000
Net Profit	35,000

(d) Compute the break-even level of output.
(e) What is your forecast of the profit for a sales volume of N160,000?
At what sales volume would a net profit of N55,000 be earned?

7. References
Dwivedi, D. N. (2002) *Managerial Economics, sixth edition* (New Delhi: Vikas Publishing House Ltd).

UNIT 18: MARKET STRUCTURE AND PRICING DECISIONS

Content
1.0 Introduction
2.0 Objectives

3.0 Market Structure and Pricing Decisions
3.1 Price Determination Under Perfect Competition
3.2 Price Determination Under Pure Monopoly
3.3 Monopoly Pricing and Output Decision in the Long-Run.
3.4 Self-Assessment Exercise
4.0 Conclusion
5.0 Summary
6.0 Tutor-Marked Assignment
7.0 References

1.0 Introduction
The market structure will determine a firm's ability to make pricing decisions or its degree of freedom in the determination of product prices. Depending on the market structure, the degree of freedom varies between zero and one. This degree of freedom implies the extent to which a firm is free or independent of the rival firm in setting product prices. The higher the degree of competition, the lower the firm's degree of freedom in making decisions about product prices. The reverse is also true.

Under *perfect competition*, a large number of firms compete against one another. It follows that the degree of competition under perfect competition is close to one. Consequently, a firm's discretion in determining the price of its product is close to zero. The firm has to accept the price determined by the market forces of demand and supply.

As the degree of competition decreases, a firm's control over the product prices and its discretion in pricing decisions increases. Under *monopolistic competition,* where the degree of competition is less than one, the firm has some discretion in product pricing.

Under oligopolistic market structure, the degree of competition is low, the firm's control over pricing decisions increases. The firms therefore, have control over the price of their products and can exercise their discretion in pricing decisions, especially where product differentiation is prominent.

2.0 Objectives
At the end of this unit, you will be able to:
1. Get acquainted with the basic principles of pricing
2. Know how to make pricing decisions under different market conditions
3. Manage consumer price expectations in an effective and efficient manner.

3.0 Market Structure and Pricing Decisions

3.1 Price Determination Under Perfect Competition
In a perfectly competitive market, commodity prices are determined by the market forces of demand and supply. In other words, market prices are determined by the market

demand and market supply, where the market demand refers to the industry demand as a whole: this is the sum of quantity demanded by each individual consumer or user of the product at different prices. Similarly, market supply is the sum of quantity supplied by individual firms in the industry. The market price is determined for the industry and the individual firms and consumers take the market price as given. This is the reason sellers under a perfectly competitive market is referred to as *price takers*.

The main problem facing a profit-maximising firm is therefore, not to determine the price of its product but to adjust its output its output to the market price so that profit is maximised.

The determination of commodity as well as services price under perfectly-competitive conditions are often analysed under three different time periods:
(i) the market period or *very short-run*;
(ii) short-run; and,
(iii) long-run.

3.1.1 Pricing in Market Period.
In market period, it is assumed the total output of a given product is fixed. Each firm in the industry has a stock of commodity or services to be sold. The stock of goods and services in the industry makes the industry supply. With the assumption of fixed stock of goods and services, the industry supply curve is perfectly inelastic, as indicated by the line SQ in figure 3.1.1 below. Given this condition of inelasticity, the price is determined solely by the condition of demand. Supply in this case is an inactive agent of price determination as it is fixed at some level of output, Q.

Figure 3.1.1: Demand - Determined Price in Market Period

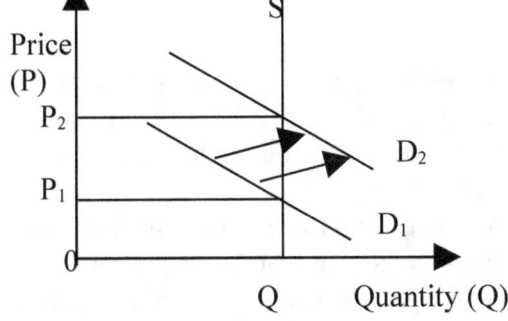

Similarly, given a fixed demand for a product or services, you will have the case of supply-determined rather than demand-determined price. This is illustrated in figure 3.1.2 below.

Figure 3.1.2: Supply-Determined Price in the Market Period

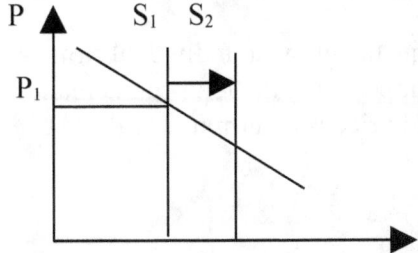

P₂ ——— D
   →
         Q₁ Q₂   Output (Q)

Pricing in the Short-Run. By definition, a short-run refers to the period in which firms can neither change their size nor quit, nor can new firms enter the industry. While in the market period, supply is absolutely fixed, in the short-run, it is possible to increase or decrease the supply by increasing or decreasing the variable inputs. In the short-run, therefore, supply curve is elastic.

The determination of market price in the short-run is illustrated by figures 3.1.3 (a) and 3.1.3 (b). Figure 3.1.3 (a) shows the determination of output based on market-determined price in figure 3.1.3 (b). This market price is fixed for all the firms in the industry.

Figure 3.1.3: Pricing in the Short-run Under Perfect Competition.

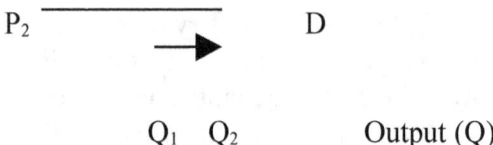

Given the industry price, P*, firms will maximise profit by equation P* to its marginal cost, MC. This can be seen from the equilibrium point E in figure 3.1.3 (a). At this point, the optimal output for the individual firm is indicated by the output level, q*.

Pricing in the Long-Run. In the long-run the firm can adjust its size or quit the industry. New firms can also enter the industry. If the market price is such that Average Revenue (AR) > Long-run Average Cost (LAC), firms will make *economic* or *super-normal* profit. As a result, new firms will enter the industry, causing a rightward shift in the supply curve. Similarly, if AR < LAC, firms will begin to make losses. In this case, marginal firms will exit the industry, causing a leftward shift in the supply curve. The rightward shift in the supply curve pulls down the market price and its leftward shift pushes it up. This process continues until price is so determined that AR = LAC and firms will now earn only normal profit.

The long-run price determination and output (or size) adjustment by an individual firm are presented in figures 3.1.4 (a) and 3.1.4 (b) below. Suppose that the long-run demand curve is represented by D_L; the short-run supply is S_1, and price is determined at P_1. At this price, firms adjust their output to the point, M, the equilibrium point, where $P_1 = AR_1 = MR_1 = LMC$. This enables firms to make economic profit of MS per unit of output. This super-normal profit lures new firms into the industry. Consequently, the industry supply curve shifts rightward to S_2, causing a fall in price to P_2. At this price, firms are in a position to cover only the long-run marginal cost (LMC) at the output q_2. At this point they will be making losses because AR < LAC. Firms incurring losses cannot survive in the long-run. Such firms will thus quit the industry. As a result, total industry production decreases, causing a leftward shift in the supply curve, to the position of S_o, for example, with the corresponding market price at P_o. The existing firms then adjust their outputs to the new market price at the output q_o. At this output, firms are in a position to make only normal profit, where $P_0 = AR = MR = LMC = LAC$, the industry equilibrium position or point. At this point, no firm is in a position to make economic profit, nor does a firm make losses.

Figure 3.1.4: Pricing in the Long-Run Under Perfect Competition

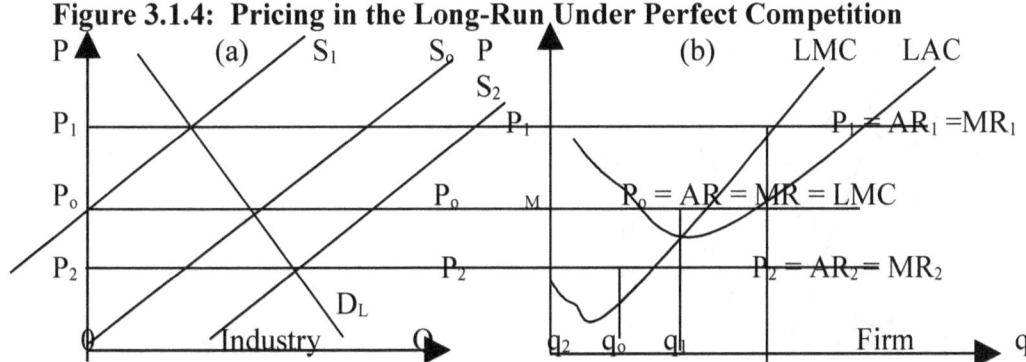

3.2 Price Determination Under Pure Monopoly

The term ***pure monopoly*** connotes absolute power to produce and sell a product with no close substitute. A monopoly market is one in which there is only on seller of a product having no close substitute. The cross-elasticity of demand for a monopolist's product is either zero or negative. A monopolized industry refers to a *single-firm* industry.

3.2.1 Monopoly Pricing and Output Decision in the Short-Run.

As in the case of perfect competition, pricing and output decision under monopoly are based on revenue and cost conditions. The cost conditions (AC and MC curves) are same for both perfect competition and pure monopoly. The difference is basically in the revenue conditions (AR and MR curves). This is so because, unlike the competitive firm, a monopoly firm faces a downward-sloping demand curve. A monopolist can reduce its product price and sell more, and raise its product price and still retain some customers.

When a demand curve slopes downward, the associated marginal revenue (MR) curve lies below the average revenue (AR) curve, and the slope of the MR curve is two times the slope of the AR curve.

The revenue and cost conditions faced by a monopoly firm in the short-run are presented in figure 3.2.1 below. The monopoly average and marginal revenue curves are represented by AR and MR curves, respectively. The short-run average and marginal cost curves are represented by SAC and SMC curves, respectively. The price and output decision rule for a profit-maximising monopolist is same as that of a firm under perfect competition. The profit-maximising monopoly firm chooses a price-output combination at which MR = SMC. Given the monopolist's cost and revenue curves in figure 3.2.1, its MR and SMC intersect each other at point E. An ordinate drawn from point E to the X-axis determines the profit-maximising level of output for the firm at Q*. At this output, firms' MR = SMC. Given the demand curve, AR = D, the output, Q* can be sold in a given time at only one price, P*. It follows that the determination of output simultaneously determines the price for the monopoly firm. For any given price, the unit and total profits are also simultaneously determined. This defines the equilibrium condition for the monopoly firm.

Figure 3.2.1: Short-Run Price Determination Under Monopoly

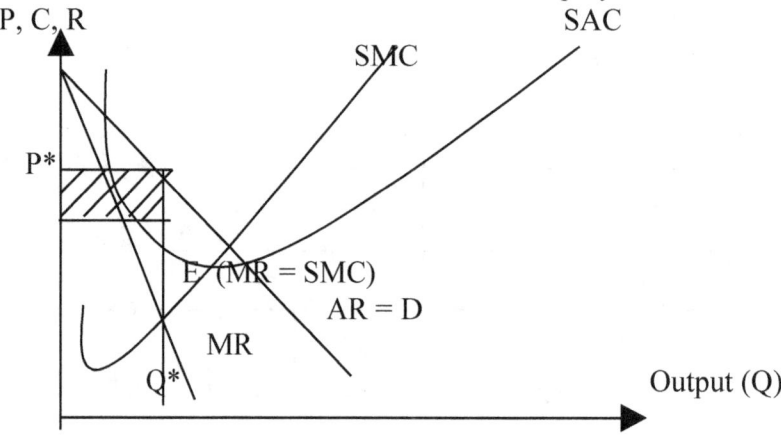

The Algebraic Determination of Monopoly Price and Output
Suppose demand and cost functions for a monopoly firm are given as:

Demand function: $Q = 100 - 0.2P$ (3.2.1)

Price function: $P = 500 - 5Q$ (3.2.2)

Cost function: $C = 50 + 20Q + Q^2$ (3.2.3)

The problem is to determine the profit-maximising level of output and price. This can be solved in the following way.

Recall that profit is maximised at an output for which MR = MC. The first step is therefore to find MR and MC using the demand and cost functions as given in equations (3.2.1) and (3.2.3), and formulate the revenue function using equations (3.2.2):

Total Revenue (R) = PQ, so that,

$R = (500 - 5Q)Q = 500Q - 5Q^2$ (3.2.4)

$$MR = \frac{dR}{dQ} = 500 - 10Q$$

Similarly,

$$MC = \frac{dC}{dQ} = 20 + 2Q$$

Equating MR to MC, the profit-maximising condition, we get:

MR = 500 − 10Q
MC = 20 + 2Q, and,

500 − 10Q = 20 + 2Q

480 = 12Q

Q* = 40.

It follows that the profit-maximising level of output is Q* = 40 units.

The profit-maximising price can be obtained by substituting Q* = 40 in the price function, equation (3.2.2) to get:

P* = 500 − 5(40) = 300.

Thus, the profit-maximising price, P* = N300.

With these information, the total (maximum) profit can be calculated as follows:

Profit (π) = R − C

$\quad$ = 500Q − 5Q² − (50 + 20Q + Q²)

$\quad$ = 500Q − 5Q² − 50 − 20Q − Q²

$\quad$ = 480Q − 6Q² − 50

Substituting for Q = 40, we obtain:

Π = 480(40) − 6(40)² − 50

$\quad$ = 19200 − 9600 − 50

$\quad$ = 9550.

Thus, the maximum profit (π^*) = N9,550.

3.3 Monopoly Pricing and Output Decision in the Long-Run.

The decision rules guiding optimal output and pricing in the long-run is same as in the short-run. In the long-run however, a monopolist gets an opportunity to expand the size of its firm with the aim of enhancing the long-run profits. Expansion of the plant size may, however, be subject to such conditions as:
   (a) the market size;
   (b) expected economic profit; and,
   (c) risk of inviting legal restrictions.

All things being equal, the equilibrium monopoly price and output determination in the long-run is illustrated by figure 3.3.1 below. According to the figure 3.3.1, the AR and MR curves show the market demand and marginal revenue conditions facing the monopolist. The long-run average cost (LAC) and the long-run marginal cost (LMC) curves indicate the long-run cost conditions. As you can observe from figure 3.3.1, the monopolist's LMC and MR intersect at point P, where output is represented as Q*. This represents the profit-maximising level of output. Given the AR curve, the price at which the output, Q* is represented by P*. It follows that, in the long-run, the monopolist output will be Q* and price, P*. This output-price combination will maximise the long-run profit. The total profit is shown by the shaded area.

Figure 3.3.1: Monopoly Equilibrium in the Long-Run.

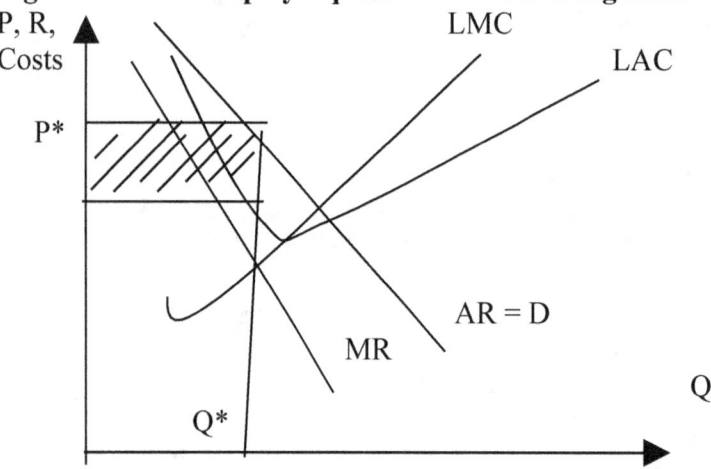

3.4 Self-Assessment Exercise

1(a) Distinguish between market period, short-run, and short-run. Does the consideration of period affect the pricing policy of a firm?

(b) Can a monopolist charge any price for its product? Give reasons for your answer.

4.0 Conclusion

The market structure will determine a firm's ability to make pricing decisions or its degree of freedom in the determination of product prices. Depending on the market structure, the degree of freedom varies between zero and one.
The main problem facing a profit-maximising firm is not to determine the price of its product but to adjust its output to the market price so that profit is maximised.

The determination of commodity as well as services price under perfectly-competitive conditions are often analysed under three different time periods:
(i) the market period or *very short-run*;
(ii) short-run; and,
(iii) long-run
As with perfect competition, pricing and output decision under monopoly are based on revenue and cost conditions. The cost conditions (AC and MC curves) are same for both perfect competition and pure monopoly. The difference is basically in the revenue conditions (AR and MR curves).

5.0 Summary
You have just been informed by this unit that:
1. In a perfectly competitive market, commodity prices are determined by the market forces of demand and supply.
2. The determination of commodity as well as services price under perfectly-competitive conditions are often analysed under three different time periods:
(i) the market period or *very short-run*;
(ii) short-run; and,
(iii) long-run.
3. As in the case of perfect competition, pricing and output decision under monopoly are based on revenue and cost conditions. A monopoly price is basically determined by equating marginal revenue (MR) to marginal cost (MC).
4. The decision rules guiding optimal output and pricing in the long-run is same as in the short-run. In the long-run however, a monopolist gets an opportunity to expand the size of its firm with the aim of enhancing the long-run profits. Expansion is sometimes subject to such conditions as:
    (d) the market size;
    (e) expected economic profit; and,
    (f) risk of inviting legal restrictions.

6.0 Tutor-Marked Assignment
A monopoly firm wishes to supply two different markets, 1 and 2, with the corresponding demand functions given as:

$P_1 = 500 - Q_1$ (Market 1)

$P_2 = 300 - Q_2$ (Market 2)

P_1 and P_2 represent the prices charged in markets 1 and 2, respectively, and Q_1 and Q_2 are quantities sold in markets 1 and 2, respectively.

The cost function is given by:

$$C = 50,000 - 100Q$$

Find:
(a) The profit maximising output for the monopolist
(b) Allocation of output between the two markets
(c) The price charged in each of the two markets
(d) The total or maximum profit.

7.0 References
1. Dwivedi, D. N. (2002) *Managerial Economics, sixth edition* (New Delhi: Vikas Publishing House Ltd).

2. Haessuler, E. F. and Paul, R. S. (1976), *Introductory Mathematical Analysis for Students of Business and Economics, 2nd edition* (Reston Virginia: Reston Publishing Company)